*Journey*

—— WITH THE ——

# APOSTLE PAUL

SIXTY DEVOTIONS

# MICHAEL GREEN

WITH ELSPETH TAYLOR

ZONDERVAN™

GRAND RAPIDS, MICHIGAN 49530 USA

# ZONDERVAN™

*A Prayer Journey with the Apostle Paul*
Copyright © 2004 by Michael Green

Requests for information should be addressed to:

Zondervan, *Grand Rapids, Michigan 49530*

Michael Green asserts the moral right to be identified as the author of this work.

A catalogue record for this book is available from the British Library.

---

**Library of Congress Cataloging-in-Publication Data**

Green, Michael, 1930-
    A prayer journey with the Apostle Paul: sixty devotions / Michael
Green with Elspeth Taylor.
      p. cm.
    ISBN 0-310-25246-6 (softcover)
    1. Prayer—Biblical teaching—Meditations.    2. Bible. N.T. Epistles of
Paul—Meditations.    3. Bible. N.T. Acts—Meditations.    I. Taylor,
Elspeth.    II. Title.
BS2655.P73G74 2004
225.9'2—dc22

          2004002603

---

*Interior design by Michelle Espinoza*

*Printed in the United States of America*

---

04 05 06 07 08 09 10 /❖ DC/ 10 9 8 7 6 5 4 3 2 1

# Contents

### Paul's Prayer

### Paul's Contemplation

## Part 6: Meditation and Adoration

### Paul's Meditation

### Paul's Petition

### Paul's Adoration

# Preface

I began to write this book out of sheer fascination. I have to confess to being an activist, and it is perfectly obvious from the pages of the New Testament that the apostle Paul was an activist as well. The trouble with activists is that they tend to do rather than to pray. I know that is shamefully true of me. But in the apostle Paul I find a man who is not only astonishingly active, serving his Lord all over the Mediterranean basin, but who is also a contemplative and a real model of intercessory prayer. I wanted to explore how he combined these two important aspects of his spiritual journey – for my own benefit and perhaps that of other activists! I became amazed at the way this man remembered in prayer so many people, and even prayed in depth for believers he had never met.

The research behind this book has been a real challenge and a great blessing to me. I hope that in the remainder of my life I may profit more from the example of this passionate, prayerful Christian leader.

## The God in Whom Paul Believed

In the pages that follow we will be looking at some of the prayers of St Paul, written in his letters. We are allowed, so to speak, to overhear the man in communion with his God. What drove Paul to such unremitting and confident prayer? I suspect the answer is the God in whom he believed.

Nearly everyone believes in a God of some sort. Some have faith in a mysterious force that set the world going, if nothing more than that. That was not the God to whom Paul prayed. Many people see God as so far removed from us that he could not possibly bother about our concerns. That was not the God to whom Paul prayed. An increasing number of people these days identify God with the natural world in which we live, and see the mountains and seas, the flowers and the birds, and above all ourselves, as divine. That was not the God to whom Paul prayed.

Paul's God was much greater and more wonderful than any of these understandings of the divine. Both in his days as a Pharisee and in his days as a Christian, Paul was a passionate believer in personal ethical monotheism:

*Personal* – doubtless God is beyond personality, but he is at least personal since he is the Creator of persons like ourselves.

*Ethical* – he cares deeply about right and wrong: he is the moral ruler of the world.

*Monotheism* – God is the single ultimate source of everything in the universe.

That is the God in whom Paul believed and to whom he prayed. He was confident that this God was transcendent – beyond our world of time and space – but also imminent – within every flower and person and sunset. Paul's God is beyond us but also alongside us. He is the God who has the power to act, because he is so great; the God who completely understands, because he is intimately involved with the world he has made and the people within it.

We could unpack Paul's belief a little further. Here are eight aspects of the God to whom he prays, which stand out clearly in Paul's writings.

## The God Who Creates

Paul is convinced that God is the Creator of the universe, and that all who do not deliberately suppress that knowledge are aware of the fact, "since what may be known about God is plain to them, because God has made it plain to them. For since the creation of the world God's invisible qualities – his eternal power and divine nature – have been clearly seen, being understood from what has been made" (Rom. 1:19–20).

## The God Who Reveals

"From infancy," he writes to his young lieutenant Timothy, "you have known the holy Scriptures, which are able to make you wise for salvation through faith in Christ Jesus. All Scripture is God-breathed and is useful for teaching, rebuking, correcting and training in righteousness, so all God's people may be thoroughly equipped for every good work" (2 Tim. 3:15–17). We are not left to grope after God in the dark. He has shown his hand.

## The God of Israel

Paul's God was not newly invented. He is the God of Abraham, Isaac and Jacob, the God worshipped and adored by the Jewish people. Paul never goes back on that conviction. "Theirs is the adoption; theirs the divine glory, the covenants, the receiving of the law, the temple worship and the promises . . . from them is traced the human ancestry of the Messiah, who is God over all, for ever praised" (Rom. 9:4–5). It is this profound sense of continuity with all that God has been doing with Israel down the centuries that enables him to congratulate Gentile believers for being descendants of Abraham: "you are all one in Christ Jesus. If you belong to Christ, then you are Abraham's seed, and heirs according to the promise" (Gal. 3:28–29).

## The God Who Came in Christ

The God Paul worships is no careless absentee who set the world going and then lost interest in it. Despite the fact that, as Paul puts it, men "did not think it worthwhile to retain the knowledge of God" (Rom. 1:28), God came in person to find us. He came as a man among men. His name was Jesus, "Who, being in very nature God, did not consider equality with God something to be used to his own advantage; rather he made himself nothing . . . being made in human likeness. And being found in appearance as a human being, he humbled himself by becoming obedient to death – even death on a cross" (Phil. 2:6–8). That is how much God cares for us.

## The God Who Saves

God came to rescue us from the fatal predicament into which we had fallen as a result of our stupid self-centredness. We rested under the "curse" of his judgment and, to Paul's endless wonder, "Christ redeemed us from the curse of the law [which we had broken] by becoming a curse for us" (Gal. 3:13). Yes, "there is one God and one mediator between God and human beings, Christ Jesus, himself human, who gave himself as a ransom for all people" (1 Tim. 2:5–6). Paul could come with utter confidence to God in prayer, knowing that he was accepted because of Christ. "We have peace with God through our Lord Jesus Christ, through whom we have gained access" (Rom. 5:1–2).

## The God Who Indwells

Paul is fundamentally confident in prayer because he knows that his God is not far off; he is not extinguished by the cross, but is alive in the hearts of believers. "If anyone does not have the Spirit of Christ, they do not belong to Christ" (Rom. 8:9). The Spirit is that part of the Godhead who dwells in the lives of believers and helps them to pray. "We do not know what we ought to pray for, but the Spirit himself intercedes for us through wordless groans. And he who searches our hearts knows the mind of the Spirit, because the Spirit intercedes for God's people in accordance with the will of God" (Rom. 8:26–27).

## The God Who Judges

Paul is well aware that God remains the Judge in his world. He looks to "the day when God judges everyone's secrets through Jesus Christ" (Rom. 2:16). And although the Christian is accepted in Christ and will not be finally lost, there remains a day of reckoning for Christians too: "For we must all appear before the judgment seat of Christ" (2 Cor. 5:10). This keeps the apostle humble and serious in his prayers. He never takes the mercy of God for granted.

## The God Who Awaits

At the end of the road there is the waiting Father. He will never scrap what is precious to him. "Now there is in store for me the crown of righteousness, which the Lord, the righteous Judge, will award to me on that day – and not only to me, but also to all who have longed for his appearing" (2 Tim. 4:8). That gives Paul enormous joy in his life and confidence in his prayers. "For I am convinced that neither death nor life, neither angels nor demons, neither the present nor the future, nor any powers, neither height nor depth, nor anything else in all creation, will be able to separate us from the love of God that is in Christ Jesus our Lord" (Rom. 8:38–39).

If that is the sort of God you believe in, it gives you enormous confidence to pray, does it not? It certainly did to Paul.

I want to end this preface with a note of deep gratitude to Amy Boucher Pye of Zondervan who conceived the idea of this book, and to Elspeth Taylor who did so much to shape it into a *A Prayer Journey with the Apostle Paul*. I hope it may be a small contribution to the vast literature on prayer, and may actually encourage us to pray!

Michael Green
Oxford, England
August 2003

# PART 1

# The Example of Paul's Prayer Life

# God's Model in Acts

## DAY 1: A PRAYER LIFE EXAMINED

When Paul had finished speaking, he knelt down ... and
prayed.

Acts 20:36

What an embarrassing place to start! How intimate. We
do not like to reveal our prayer life to anybody else. To be
sure, we will talk about prayer until the cows come home. We
will cheerfully join in public prayer in church, or pray informally
in the prayer meeting, perhaps; but to allow our practice of private prayer to be observed by someone else is a different matter.

What if they discover how barren and empty I am feeling,
inside the cheery outer appearance? What if they find out how
rarely I pray, and how perfunctory it often is? No, I would not
like to have my personal prayer life examined, even by a close and
understanding friend. But Paul's prayer life was scrutinised in this
way, and his friend's testimony to it is even more impressive than
the references which the apostle himself makes. It is someone else
looking in, someone who could not be taken in by externals,
someone who knew Paul intimately.

That friend was Luke – Luke the doctor; Luke the companion of St Paul on many of his journeys; Luke who went through

the rigours of prison with him and the hazards of shipwreck. Now Luke does not set out in Acts to write about the prayer life of his friend, but he does let slip a number of allusions which show us that he noticed it and was moved by it. We can come alongside this beloved, faithful friend and catch some glimpses of Paul at prayer.

> *Heavenly Father, you know that I fail so often to walk closely with you in prayer. Forgive me for the times I have ignored you. Please teach me to talk with you intimately, that I may learn to rely on you fully and be guided by you. Amen.*

# DAY 2: THE SAUL WHO HAD TO BE CHANGED

> Saul was still breathing out murderous threats against the
> Lord's disciples. He went to the high priest and asked him for
> letters to the synagogues in Damascus, so that if he found any
> there who belonged to the Way, whether men or women, he
> might take them as prisoners to Jerusalem.
>
> Acts 9:1–2

Prayer does not come easily to us, does it? Almost everyone prays, atheists included, at times of stress and danger.
But few of us, Christians included, have an ease, an intimacy in
prayer such as you might expect to find in family conversation
between children and parents. We need help in this area above
almost anything else in the spiritual life. And God in his generosity has provided it. He has given us a model in prayer. "Oh,"
you say. "Some saint, some monk, insulated from the pressures
of normal life? Someone who doesn't understand the strains and
stresses I have to face?" Not at all.

In Saul of Tarsus, the persecutor who became the apostle
Paul, God has shown us someone who can help us enormously
in this matter of prayer. It did not come easily to him, either.
Saul was an activist – and activists are notoriously weak at
relaxed, meditative prayer. Saul was quick-tempered and criti-
cal – hardly the soil in which to grow the gentle plant of prayer.
Saul was an intellectual of the highest stature – with all the intellectual's determination to think his way through a problem,
rather than to pray his way through it. And Saul was proud,
proud of his nationality, his religion, his background, his wealth,
his rectitude, his competence. People like that find prayer very
difficult. They often have to be broken first. Such was the case

with Saul on the Damascus Road. You see, pride says, "My will be done," and prayer says, "Thy will be done." The two are miles apart.

God, in his goodness, chose this most unlikely man to be a model to Christians in the matter of prayer. Intellect need be no barrier to prayer. Activity need be no barrier to prayer. Temperament need be no barrier to prayer. A life on the road need be no barrier to prayer. Organisational skills need not be incompatible with a deep life of prayer; they are, in fact, disastrous without it.

Saul of Tarsus, the energetic persecutor, shows that whatever our temperament, our job, our skills, our weaknesses, God can make us men and women of prayer. I am so grateful for that. There is hope for the likes of you and me!

*Dear Lord, thank you so much for giving us Saul to show that you can transform us into people of prayer despite our weaknesses. Please soften my heart to seek and respond to your will. Amen.*

# DAY 3: SURRENDER TO GOD

> As he neared Damascus on his journey, suddenly a light from
> heaven flashed around him. He fell to the ground and heard
> a voice say to him, "Saul, Saul, why do you persecute me?"
> "Who are you, Lord?" Saul asked.
>
> "I am Jesus, whom you are persecuting," he replied.
>
> Acts 9:3–5

A story is told of Admiral Nelson after one of his victories over the French fleet. The opposing admiral came on to his quarterdeck and offered Nelson his hand. "Your sword first, sir," said Nelson. There could be no companionship until there had been explicit surrender. That is what Paul did at his conversion. He gave in to God. He admitted that God was in the right and he was not. His proud knees bowed, and he cried to God for mercy. That is when prayer first became real to him.

Paul himself later described prayer as the first fruit of reconciliation with God: "Since we have been justified through faith, we have peace with God through our Lord Jesus Christ, through whom we have gained access" (Rom. 5:1). That is it – access! The barriers are down and access is available. That is a lovely way to think of prayer. Whereas in the past there was a forbidding notice, "No Through Road", we now read the encouraging sign, "Way Clear".

We need to let the wonder of this touch us afresh. We have turned away from God, but in the wonder of the good news, God, as Karl Barth so charmingly put it, "invites us to live with him".

*Merciful God, I know that I am far from worthy of a relationship with you. I praise and thank you that you have found me, forgiven me, and made it possible for me to walk daily with you. Amen.*

# DAY 4: EVIDENCE OF NEW LIFE

> In Damascus there was a disciple named Ananias. The Lord
> called to him in a vision, "Ananias!"
>
> "Yes, Lord," he answered.
>
> The Lord told him, "Go to the house of Judas on Straight
> Street and ask for a man from Tarsus named Saul, for he is
> praying."
>
> Acts 9:10–11

*T*here is a remarkable little phrase in the story of Paul's conversion. Ananias is told by God to go and visit this fearsome enemy of the budding Christian movement. He can go without trepidation to that house in Straight Street to ask for Saul, "for he is praying". Just that, but what an eloquent phrase. It reveals so much. And it is perfectly astonishing.

A Jew's life was bathed in prayer. His orthodox Jewish parents would have conceived Saul in prayer and brought him to birth in prayer. His earliest memories would be of prayers with his mother, Friday night prayers in the home, Sabbath synagogue prayers, temple prayers at great feasts. There would be prayers at three fixed times in the day. As a Pharisee, Saul would have laid special emphasis on prayer, worn the prayer shawl and prayed publicly and out loud as befitted a "separated one" (see Matt. 6:5).

And yet he had not begun to pray! He simply said prayers. Did those prayers reach God? The Pharisee in Jesus' story "prayed about himself" (Luke 18:11). It was only when, like the tax collector, he cried "God, have mercy on me, a sinner" on the road to Damascus that he really got through to God for the first time in his life. Prayer is communion with God, and nothing hinders it as much as the proud, sinful self-centredness which is so characteristic of us all. It comes like a cloud between us and the sun. It is only when we are humble enough to come to God for his pardon that the cloud rolls away, and the light and warmth of his sunshine begin to become real to us. In other words, prayer is the fruit of getting on the right terms with God.

Real prayer is the first sign of new life with God. When Paul sketches the story of salvation in Galatians 4, he makes the believer's cry of "Abba, Father" (v. 6) the crowning evidence of sonship. It is the assurance that we belong in the family, just as the first sign of life in a baby when it is born into the world is a cry. God's children always begin to speak to him in prayer, a demonstration that the Spirit of his Son has taken up residence in our hearts and is beginning to enliven our spirit. It is perhaps the most important sign of spiritual life, just as breathing is of physical life. At all events, it is the only sign God gave to Ananias of Saul's change of heart. If our own lives were judged by that same criterion, could we hold our heads high? "He is praying." Are we?

> *Dear Father, please rid me of my self-centredness, so that I may get on the right terms with you in true submission. Let me know the light and warmth of your presence. And teach me to pray. Amen.*

# The Means of Guidance

## DAY 5: STILLED BY GOD

> In a vision he has seen a man named Ananias come and place
> his hands on him to restore his sight.
>
> Acts 9:12

There is more to learn from that tantalisingly brief reference to Saul praying in the house on Straight Street. It shows that prayer was not only the sign of life, but also the means of God's guidance. Imagine this proud, intellectual, zealous Pharisee, so used to commanding and to leading, for the first time reduced to immobility. For three days, we read, he was blind after the Damascus Road experience, and no food or water passed his lips. Just imagine it! Three days without food is more than most of us could readily face, but three days in total blindness, not knowing whether he would ever see again – that must have been a terrifying experience. It took all of that to bring Saul to a place where he would listen to God and seek his direction and his plan.

It was during this terrible time that Saul was still enough to receive God's guidance. That guidance was very specific. Saul was shown that release was at hand. He was shown the very name of the person who would bring it. He was shown the method that would be used to restore his sight. Amazing! And God showed it

all to him as he prayed. He could never have imagined those
things and got them right. He could never have planned them
with his organisational skills. God showed him, once he was
brought to the point of inner stillness and dependence.

I think of a couple who were accustomed to waiting on God
in prayer. The husband's job changed, and he needed to take his
family to another part of the country. As they contemplated the
move, his wife had a vision of the house they would live in. Well,
they went to see the town where the new job was to be and could
not find a house that seemed suitable, let alone one that resem-
bled the picture the wife had seen. On their last morning, however, they suddenly saw the very house. There was no "For Sale"
sign outside, but still they went to knock on the door. "As a matter of fact, we have put this house on the market today," the own-
ers said. But the price was far too high. My friends offered what
they could – and waited. In due course, other potential buyers
all fell by the wayside, and my friends bought it at the price they
could afford. They are happily ensconced in it today and are using
it for ministry to other people.

God gave specific guidance in this instance as they waited on
him in prayer. The God who guided Saul specifically is still in
business!

*Loving Lord, I thank you that you turned Paul around to listen
to you. Please still my heart, so that I may hear you and be guided
by you. Amen.*

# DAY 6: RECEPTIVE TO GOD

> When I returned to Jerusalem and was praying at the temple,
> I fell into a trance and saw the Lord speaking to me, "Quick!"
> he said. "Leave Jerusalem immediately, because the people here
> will not accept your testimony about me . . . Go; I will send
> you far away to the Gentiles."
>
> Acts 22:17–18, 21

*A*cts gives us two other clear examples of the apostle being guided as he prayed. One appears in Paul's own account of his conversion in chapter 22. Paul is alone in the temple, praying. Again we see here the true nature of prayer: communion with God. It is an instructive passage.

Paul, the great man of action, is also Paul, the great man of prayer. His talking *about* God is matched by his talking *to* God. On this occasion he loses all account of time: he is face to face with the Eternal. As he prays, God makes his will clear. The warning saved Paul's life. We do not know if Paul was asking about his future. At all events, a humble, receptive attitude to God in prayer made it easy for the Lord to get through to him with something Paul very much needed to hear. He was willing to obey God, cost what it might. He prayed; God guided him.

Would you like guidance about your future, your job, or where you should live? Well, we may reverently think that it is God's job to guide us, but it is our job to seek his will in an attitude of openness and obedience. He does not tell us *how* he may make his will known to us, but he *does* undertake to do it: "He guides the humble in what is right and teaches them his way" (Ps. 25:9). Prayer is the condition, the supreme condition – indeed, almost the only condition – of guidance.

*Eternal God, I thank you that you respond to the prayers of your people. Please help me to come face to face with you in prayer, ready to listen to you and open to follow your will. Amen.*

# DAY 7: WHEN WE FIGHT GOD'S WILL

Teach me your way, O LORD.

Psalm 27:11

*W*e have seen how important prayer is in allowing God to lead us, and here is a phrase from the Psalms that Paul must have used many times.

While I was wondering whether to accept a job at Regent College, Vancouver, for which there was no available finance, I found myself speaking to about seventy people in a hotel. I talked about the need for someone to teach evangelism at the college, but I resisted the idea that it should be me. As people left, one of them came up and said, "I will pay your salary." I replied, in amazement, that it was not a question of "me", but that he should go and make his offer known to the principal.

He was followed by a lady who said, "I had a picture yesterday as I was praying with a friend. It was of a grand piano. I sensed that the lovely music coming from it was the music of the gospel. The piano was open, so that it masked the face of the person playing it. Behind it was a plate-glass window. The room was large; I didn't recognise it. After this picture my friend and I happened to pray for you; you were one of eighteen people we prayed for that day. Having come to this reception today, I at once recognised the room. There was the plate-glass window. There was the piano. You tried to sit at another table, but the principal uprooted you and put you at a table with him, just in front of the grand piano. And when you got up to speak, you declined to use the podium, and spoke from just in front of the piano. I believe you are meant to come to Vancouver, and to spread the harmony of the gospel in evangelism." Well, I went, and it happened!

That was a remarkable example of God directing my future through a vision received in prayer. I fought it for a year before I gave in – and how glad I am that I did give in. The will of God is the best thing that could possibly happen to us, hard though we may find that to believe at any particular time of change in our lives!

There are many examples in the New Testament of Christians, including Paul, being guided by a vision to a course of action they would not have chosen. Think of Paul and the man of Macedonia (Acts 16:6–10). Where would Europe have been had he not acted on that?

> *Holy Lord and Father, I praise you that you long to teach me your way, as you taught the psalmist and the apostle Paul. I spend so much time and energy running in the opposite direction. Help me by your almighty power to stop fighting your will, and to give in to the best possible plan for my life. Amen.*

## Day 8: Prayer and fasting

> In the church at Antioch there were prophets and teachers:
> Barnabas, Simeon called Niger, Lucius of Cyrene, Manaen
> (who had been brought up with Herod the tetrarch) and Saul.
> While they were worshipping the Lord and fasting, the Holy
> Spirit said, "Set apart for me Barnabas and Saul for the work
> to which I have called them." So after they had fasted and
> prayed, they placed their hands on them and sent them off.
>
> Acts 13:1–3

*A* third example of God guiding Paul's life through prayer
comes in Acts 13. The scene has changed dramatically.
From the Jewish temple service we move to the Gentile church
meeting. Paul is no longer alone. He is in the midst of one of the
most remarkable churches in the ancient world, the church at
Antioch. This church, founded by wandering laymen, became
the springboard of world mission.

There was real fellowship there, no pride of place: five men
are mentioned as forming the corporate leadership of that church,
and Paul is mentioned last in the list. There was no social dis-
tinction: the group contained at least one black man and one
member of the ruling elite.

They were all intent on one thing – God's glory. They were
"worshipping" him: the word used in the Greek suggests something much more formal than the private prayer of chapter 22.
Do not despise public, formal prayer: enter into it, and learn to
use it. God can well make his way known through it.

Moreover, these Antioch Christians fasted. This is a vital
accessory to serious prayer. It tells God we love him more than
food. It tells him we mean business about prayer. We should not

have a narrow view of fasting: it may mean temporary abstinence from sleep, or sex, or sport, or TV.

It was when they fasted that God led them as a group to this new venture which would bring the gospel of Jesus out of the Jewish ghetto and into the Gentile world. God made it plain to them that they should release their two most gifted leaders to do overseas work. What a contrast this is to the modern church. How poverty-stricken our fellowship, how weak our prayer and fasting! As a result, how uncertain we are of the guidance of God, and how slow to take up imaginative initiatives.

> *Glorious Saviour, I thank you so much for my brothers and sisters in Christ with whom I can worship and seek your will. Enable us together to clear away the diversions of our lives so that we may focus on you and be guided by you to the great plans you have for us. Amen.*

# The Secret of Power

## DAY 9: STRENGTHENED BY PRAYER

> Paul and Barnabas appointed elders for them in each church
> and, with prayer and fasting, committed them to the Lord, in
> whom they had put their trust.
>
> Acts 14:23

Picture the scene: in the wilds of Turkey, on that first mem-
orable missionary journey out of Antioch, the gospel is proclaimed. The missionaries are kicked out of town, after provoking
a riot with the Jews. Some of the hearers believe; others reject the
message. So what do Paul and Barnabas do? In every church, they
ordain rivals to the synagogue leadership – and then they disap-
pear! In that case I am not at all surprised to read the previous
verse. It is an understatement that, "We must go through many
hardships to enter the kingdom of God" (v. 22).

Would you have liked to be in the shoes of one of these fledg-
ling elders? I wonder what kept them spiritually alive. They had
no senior minister to guide them, no church order or precedent
to follow, no New Testament to read, no church buildings and
no money. How did they manage to stand upright? They did it
through prayer. That is how. God strengthens us as we pray. That
is, surely, why Paul begs again and again throughout his letters,
"Brothers, pray for us."

Prayer is God's appointed channel for pouring his blessing on others. Missionaries in foreign fields and Christian friends in tough jobs are more strengthened by our prayers than we shall ever know. Some of our friends who have passed through crises will have been aware of a barrage of prayer for them just when they needed it most. But with only a very few moments spent in prayer each day, we show where our priorities lie. Is it any wonder that we see so little of the power of God, compared with our prayer-conscious brothers and sisters in Korea and Singapore, in São Paulo and Dar es Salaam?

Paul himself was wonderfully strengthened as he prayed amidst the troubles at Corinth. "Do not be afraid; keep on speaking, do not be silent. For I am with you, and no one is going to attack and harm you" (Acts 18:9–10).

*Mighty Lord, so often I forget to come to you in prayer when I most need your help. Please teach me, as you taught those early Christians, to put my trust in you so that I may see your power at work in my life and in the lives of others. Amen.*

# DAY 10: THE LIBERATING POWER OF PRAYER

> Paul and Silas were praying and singing hymns to God . . .
> Suddenly there was such a violent earthquake that the foundations of the prison were shaken. At once all the prison doors
> flew open, and everyone's chains came loose.
>
> Acts 16:25–26

*I*t is not only prayer for others that is the key to effective, fruitful Christian living. It was as Paul and Silas sang praises and uttered heartfelt prayers in a filthy Philippian prison that the earthquake took place which broke them free from their chains. Prayer was the gateway for release, and so it still is. I am sure the Philippians never forgot this amazing incident. Nor did Paul. When he was once again in prison, he wrote to the Philippians:

> I will continue to rejoice, for I know that through your prayers and God's provision of the Spirit of Jesus Christ what has happened to me will turn out for my deliverance.
>
> Phil. 1:18–19

Paul and his readers knew that they were dealing with the God of the impossible. Prayer was and is the secret weapon at our disposal: it brings down into our experience the liberating power of Almighty God. In some mysterious way, the "help given by the Spirit of Jesus Christ" is linked with humble, human prayers.

Each of us will be able to think of some personal incident when we have known the manifest power of prayer in our lives. On a broader canvas, history has shown breathtaking answers to prayer in the fall of apartheid and communist regimes.

*Almighty God, I praise you for the witness of Christians who have gone before, and for your miraculous intervention in their lives. Make me a disciple who prays humbly from the heart and sings your praises aloud. May I testify to the power of your Spirit in situations where change seems humanly impossible. Amen.*

# The Avenue for Healing

## DAY 11: THE AVENUE FOR HEALING

> [Publius] welcomed us to his home and showed us generous
> hospitality for three days. His father was sick in bed, suffering
> from fever and dysentery. Paul went in to see him and, after
> prayer, placed his hands on him and healed him.
>
> Acts 28:7–8

In the days of the New Testament, prayer, with or without the laying on of hands and with or without anointing with oil (James 5:15), was a medium through which God was pleased to bring healing. It still is, all over the world. Though initially sceptical that God would intervene to answer prayer for healing, I have seen so much of it that I can only marvel at my earlier obtuseness and unbelief.

We must beware of Christian rationalism. We are prone to turn to God in prayer for healing only as a last resort when all hope is gone. "I'm so sorry," we say, "the case seems hopeless, so perhaps we had better pray." God should never be sought as a last resort. We should come to him first and foremost, before we turn to the doctor, and put our situation in his hands and seek his purposes for us. God is the God of salvation, and time and again that word in the Scriptures embraces (indeed, very often means) "healing".

The church once again needs to be a healing community. It is a sick and broken world in which we live, with sick bodies, sick minds, sick experiences, sick relationships and sick addictions. It cries out for the healing at many levels which only God can bring, and which he has determined to channel through the prayers of his people.

> *Loving Father, forgive me for my timidity in praying for those who are sick in body, mind or spirit. I think of those I know who are suffering now and ask you to act in their lives according to your will and power, for the sake of your kingdom. Amen.*

# DAY 12: GOD'S POWER IN OUR WEAKNESS

> I was given a thorn in my flesh . . . Three times I pleaded with the Lord to take it away from me. But he said to me, "My grace is sufficient for you, for my power is made perfect in weakness."
>
> 2 Corinthians 12:7–9

While God can and does intervene in answer to prayer – giving us a foretaste of the glory that shall be hereafter, when neither sin nor suffering will mar his creation – it is salutary to step into one of Paul's letters for a moment and recall that the agony from which he himself suffered, his "thorn in the flesh" (almost certainly a physical ailment), was not healed. Paul also had to leave his sick friend Trophimus at Miletus (2 Tim. 4:20).

We must beware of making exaggerated claims about Christian healing. God does not always heal when prayer is made. We live in a fallen world, where God does not eradicate all suffering any more than he eradicates all sin.

God had other plans for Paul, and he had to trust that they were for the greater good. In response to Paul's prayerful pleading, God assured him that his power was made perfect in such weakness and that his grace would be sufficient for whatever Paul had to endure. Paul took this answer to heart, and thereafter vowed to be glad of his weaknesses, so that Christ's power might rest on him.

We must never be callous about the illnesses and sufferings that many endure, but in our own lives we can pray for God's grace in the face of suffering, knowing that we will be made strong in Christ when we are weak in worldly terms. Indeed, it is sometimes when we are stripped bare by the deepest pain that we truly fall to our knees in prayer and experience God most fully, aware that he is our only strength.

> *Gracious Lord and Creator, you are pained by our sufferings more than we can know, and sometimes we are overwhelmed by all that is wrong around us. May we always remember your sovereign power which is greatest in our weakness. Please give us peace and strength to endure in the knowledge of the hope we have in you. Amen.*

# The Expression of Fellowship

## DAY 13: PRAYER THAT FORGES DEEP BONDS

> We sought out the disciples there and stayed with them seven
> days . . . When it was time to leave, we left and continued on
> our way. All of them, including wives and children, accompa-
> nied us out of the city, and there on the beach we knelt to pray.
>
> Acts 21:4–5

After only a week's acquaintance with the Christians at
Tyre (on his way from Ephesus to Jerusalem), what do we
find as Paul comes to say farewell? He prays with all his brothers
and sisters in Christ, just as he had after three years' intensive
ministry among the Ephesians (Acts 20:36).

It is the supreme way for Christian love to flow. It is the
fastest way for brothers and sisters in Christ to go deep with one
another. It is the universal language. You can pray with a group
of Christians whose language you cannot understand. No matter:
you will have gone deep with them, and a bond will have been
forged that is too deep for words. Let us never get beyond praying with one another. Some Christians, to their loss, have never
begun to experience it. It is the most natural, as well as the most
profound, expression of fellowship between members of the same
family.

Prayer between believers is nothing to be pompous about; there is no need to draw attention to ourselves. I think of a knot of friends in a tight circle in Durban airport, lost in prayer and only just making the flight after an insistent last call through the PA system!

Of course, such naturalness could degenerate into over-familiarity. There is no sign of this in Paul. When he said his departing prayers with his friends, we read that he knelt. Now, the Bible is not fussy about posture in prayer. Standing is normal ("when you stand praying..."), sitting is fine ("David sat before the Lord..."), and sometimes, I am glad to read, "the saints rejoiced in their beds"! But kneeling has something that the Protestant crouch can never equal. It is an expression of deep humility before the sovereign Lord, our Maker.

Yes, prayer is the supreme expression of fellowship. Let us value it and use it corporately, as Paul did: praying together in the home, in small church groups, away on vacation. It is the communion of redeemed sons and daughters with their Creator who is also their Father. Both intimacy and respect are required of us. And he longs for us to come to him *together* to pray.

*Dear Lord, I praise you for the fellowship of praying with others, as we express our oneness in you. Please show me how to use this gift more valuably – with those I pray with already, or in finding new prayer partners – so that our intimacy in prayer may bring us closer to you. Amen.*

# DAY 14: A PRAYER FOR TIMOTHY

> To Timothy, my dear son: Grace, mercy and peace from God
> the Father and Christ Jesus our Lord. I thank God . . . as night
> and day I constantly remember you in my prayers. Recalling
> your tears, I long to see you, so that I may be filled with joy.
> I have been reminded of your sincere faith, which first lived in
> your grandmother Lois and in your mother Eunice and, I am
> persuaded, now lives in you also. For this reason I remind you
> to fan into flame the gift of God.
>
> 2 Timothy 1:1–6

*N*ot many of Paul's prayers for individuals are recorded,
but those we do have provide us with four poignant inter-
ludes in our readings.

In this last and most intimate of Paul's letters we see him at
prayer for someone he loved deeply, Timothy. He had led Timothy
to faith, worked with him on many evangelistic forays, and been
in prison with him. Now, himself in prison once more, Paul writes
to this trusted lieutenant to encourage him in his role of leadership. The normal convention in ancient letters was to write, "A to
B, greeting" (Greek) or "A to B, peace be with you" (Hebrew). But
Paul is not bound by convention. He combines the Greek "grace"
with the Hebrew "peace" and throws in, for good measure,
"mercy". God offers his grace for all our daily needs; he offers us his
deep, enfolding peace; but above all we stand only because of his
mercy to sinners like us. Paul never forgot it, either for himself or
for experienced Christians like Timothy.

This prayer is tinged with gratitude and memory. Paul is so
thankful for his beloved Timothy. As he prays the years roll back,
and he recalls Timothy's home life – the Jewish maternal side of

the family and the pagan paternal side (Acts 16:1ff). He is so grateful for the Jewish heritage, for the faith that enlivened at least one half of the family; grateful for the tears (perhaps indicative of the struggle between the believer and the pagan in Timothy's teenage heart?); grateful for the faith that had come to mark him, grateful for the gift of God which indwelt Timothy, the Holy Spirit himself. He allows memory and imagination to prompt him into praise and thanksgiving: "I constantly remember you in my prayers." Mental imagery of someone or something we are praying for is an important element in the life of prayer, directing us into sensitive intercession. Only after remembering, thanking and praying does Paul remind Timothy of what he needs to keep in mind. It is a pattern we could well adopt in our concern for those we love.

Paul is imprisoned in very tough circumstances, possibly in the Mamertime prison in Rome – a real hellhole – and "night and day" probably reflects the pain, sleeplessness and cold to which he was exposed. How easy it would have been to give way to fruitless frustration. Instead he turned those wakeful hours into the fruitful channel of prayer. We can do a great deal of praying when we cannot get to sleep, asking the Lord what he wants to teach us by the sleeplessness – perhaps to re-establish our focus on him, and then asking for whom he wants us to pray.

*Faithful Lord, I thank you for friends and family who are so precious to me. I think of the ways that you have worked in their lives, and ask that you will continue to bring them to know more of your grace, mercy and peace each day. Amen.*

# PART 2

# The Priority
# of Prayer
# in Paul's Letters

# A Major Component
# of the Epistles

## DAY 15: PRAYER BUBBLING AT THE SURFACE

Grace and peace to you from God our Father and the Lord Jesus Christ, who gave himself for our sins to rescue us from the present evil age, according to the will of our God and Father, to whom be glory for ever and ever. Amen.

Galatians 1:3–5

*I* am amazed at the constant incidental glimpses of Paul at prayer which confront us in his letters. In every one of his epistles we see something of this incredible man at prayer. There are no exceptions. It is not a prominent theme in Titus, a letter on church leadership to one of his lieutenants, but it is there at beginning and end (Titus 1:4; 3:15). It is not prominent in Galatians, a letter written in anger at the church being swamped by legalism on one side and libertinism on the other; but it forms the framework (Gal. 1:3–5; 6:16, 18).

In all of Paul's other letters prayer is either a massive component, as in Ephesians, or at least a substantial one. I find the stress on prayer remarkable in this maverick, activist, choleric Jew who dashed all over the known world – when he was not languishing in prison. For him, prayer is a priority, whether he is writing to Timothy, who led a chain of churches, or to Philemon, his rich, landowning convert who led a house church.

It makes no difference whether he is writing to an encouraging church like Philippi, or a somewhat discouraging one like Corinth; whether he is writing to people he knew well like the Philippians, or people he had never met like the Colossians. And when he is writing two general letters, both of which seem to have been intended for wider circulation, i.e. Romans and Ephesians, prayer comes bubbling to the surface in a big way. It is truly astonishing.

> *Loving Lord and Father, I thank you that the life and letters of your servant Paul show that prayer is of the utmost priority. Please ignite my heart to have such a passion for conversing with you that prayer may mark my every step, for the sake of your glory. Amen.*

# *Filled with God's Grace*

## Day 16: The theme which dominated Paul's life

> I thank Christ Jesus our Lord, who has given me strength, that he considered me trustworthy, appointing me to his service. Even though I was once a blasphemer and a persecutor and a violent man, I was shown mercy because I acted in ignorance and unbelief. The grace of our Lord was poured out on me abundantly, along with the faith and love that are in Christ Jesus.
>
> 1 Timothy 1:12–14

It was grace which brought Paul to God in the first place: sheer undeserved favour from the Lord himself to an arrogant, undeserving Pharisee. Paul had an ever-deepening awareness of it. It was grace which called him, though he was not fit to be ranked an apostle (1 Cor. 15:9–11). It was grace which drove him to his knees in awe and wonder that even he could be useful to God in proclaiming the story of his mercy to those who had never heard it (Eph. 3:8). And it was the grace of God which became more and more precious to him the older he grew. It comes to a crescendo in this, one of his last letters:

Christ Jesus came into the world to save sinners – of whom I am the worst. But for that very reason I was shown mercy so that in me, the worst of sinners, Christ Jesus might display his immense patience as an example for those who would believe on him and receive eternal life. Now to the King eternal, immortal, invisible, the only God, be honor and glory for ever and ever. Amen.

1 Tim. 1:15–17

That is the theme which dominated his life – the undeserved generosity of God. He knows himself to be utterly undeserving in God's sight, and yet the Lord has had mercy on him and has entrusted him with the task of making known to others this undreamed-of offer of free acceptance by the God we have all wronged. "The worst of sinners" – but rescued in order to be an example for those who would believe across the world and down the centuries. No wonder he erupts in praise!

*Gracious Lord, I praise you that you have shown me such unde-served favour, in spite of my rebellion, and that you long to use me in your service. I ask that I may never take your grace for granted, but may live a life worthy of such a calling. Amen.*

# Day 17: Prayer centred on the grace of God

Because of his great love for us, God, who is rich in mercy, made us alive with Christ even when we were dead in transgressions – it is by grace you have been saved.

Ephesians 2:4–5

It was grace which Paul's congregations needed as much as he did, so that, above all else, is what he prays for. We find it at the start of his letters: "Grace and peace to you from God our Father and the Lord Jesus Christ" (1 Cor. 1:3); and we find it at the end of his letters: "The grace of the Lord Jesus Christ be with your spirit" (Philem. v. 25). From first to last the Christian life is one of experiencing God's grace. Prayer is the instrument God delights to use in order to enable people to grasp his goodness.

Grace has a many-sided splendour. When believers come to God in the first instance, it is grace, perceived as unmerited favour, which accepts them – it is by grace that we are saved. "Grace" here manifestly means the undeserved acceptance of sinful people like us by the God who owes us nothing, but loves us just the same. In prayer for others, there is no higher thing we could pray for than that they may come to appreciate this in their own lives.

Often, as above, Paul joins "peace" with "grace" in his prayers for his friends, longing that this peace of God will mark the lives of those in whom his grace is active. Always grace is central to Paul's prayers: it made a new man of him. That is his supreme desire for his churches and the individuals within them. All we need is more of the grace of God, the generous God who gives himself continuously to us, in order to meet our varied needs.

*Dear Lord, I honour and praise you for the gift of your grace, by which you have turned my life around and made me a new person. I ask that those who are dear to me in Christ will grasp this truth for themselves. I pray that we may know your peace in our hearts, as we experience such profound love and mercy. Amen.*

# DAY 18: STRENGTH AND GRACIOUSNESS

> He said to me, "My grace is sufficient for you, for my power
> is made perfect in weakness." Therefore I will boast all the
> more gladly about my weaknesses, so that Christ's power may
> rest on me.
>
> 2 Corinthians 12:9

The sheer unmerited grace of God takes on other shades
of meaning in Paul's writing. One of them is "strength".
Once believers have come to appreciate what God has done in
saving and accepting us, we are called to a life of progressive holi-
ness, just as our heavenly Father is holy. But this is beyond the
power of human beings, prone as we are to slip and fall. What
we need if we are ever to begin to live the Christian life is the
Lord's "grace", his power to overcome the downward forces which
plague us.

There is a resulting dimension to grace, "graciousness": "Let
your conversation be always full of grace, seasoned with salt, so
that you may know how to answer everyone" (Col. 4:6).

One of the manifest marks of the Lord's strength in our lives
comes precisely here, in our way of life, particularly our conversation: if we really are drawing on his strength, we shall exhibit a
new graciousness in the way we talk to others. Undeserved love
accepting us just as we are; undeserved strength enabling us to
live for him; and unexpected graciousness in speech as the love
and power of the Lord begin to grip us and work through us.
What higher thing could Paul have prayed for in his converts
than grace?

*Almighty Lord, I thank you that your grace takes my frailty and makes it your strength. I pray for those I know who are going through tough times, that they may know your sustaining power. I ask that you will give me gracious words that are a witness to your transforming power. Amen.*

# The Focus of Paul's Prayers

## DAY 19: PRAYER FOR CHRISTLIKENESS

> We constantly pray for you, that our God may make you worthy of his calling, and that by his power he may bring to fruition your every desire for goodness and your every deed prompted by faith. We pray this so that the name of our Lord Jesus may be glorified in you, and you in him, according to the grace of our God and the Lord Jesus Christ.
>
> 2 Thessalonians 1:11–12

If the prayers of an average modern Christian were to undergo scrutiny, we would be likely to find that prayer for specific things predominates. Prayer for health, for financial needs, for success in examinations, sport or career. These concerns are strikingly absent from the apostle's prayers, though he was exposed to such a variety of hardships that we might have imagined that they would be prominent.

His concern for his friends was not so much the meeting of particular physical and emotional needs but growth in maturity and Christlikeness. Thus he prays that his troublesome followers in Thessalonica will be made worthy of God's calling, growing in faith and their desire for goodness. He wants the Philippians to grow in love, discernment and the fruitfulness of a blameless

Christian life (Phil. 1:9–11). Like his friend Epaphras, he prays for his readers to become mature and assured, standing firm in all the will of God (Col. 4:12).

If Christians learnt to do this more often, there would be less complaining at the failure of God to answer our prayers. He is not some heavenly superstore to supply our shopping lists. He is the high and holy one who inhabits eternity, bent on preparing his children to share it with him for ever. He wants us to "be conformed to the likeness of his Son" (Rom. 8:29).

*Holy Lord, I thank you that you want to live and work in a heart like mine. Please transform my desires to mirror those of your Son, Christ Jesus, my Saviour. I pray for those I know who are struggling with their Christian walk, that you would help them to grow in faith, so that together we may be prepared for eternity. Amen.*

# DAY 20: PRAYER FOR EVERY ASPECT OF OUR LIVES

> Do not be anxious about anything, but in every situation, by prayer and petition, with thanksgiving, present your requests to God. And the peace of God, which transcends all understanding, will guard your hearts and your minds in Christ Jesus.
>
> Philippians 4:6–7

Paul did not indulge in the "shopping list" type of prayer. Neither did he engage in banal generalities in his prayers. They were designed for the maturing of his readers and the glory of God, but at the same time they addressed very specific situations. If our prayers are vague, we shall never notice any response to them.

On the personal scale, we find in Paul's writings prayers for peace of mind in the midst of worry, as above. On the international scale, we find prayers for the leaders of nations: not only for themselves, but that by good government they would help to induce a climate of peace, godliness and mutual respect. Happy the country so governed!

In his own life, we find prayers for travel plans: Paul expects Philemon's prayers to be effective for his release (Philem. v. 22). We find prayers that he be delivered from violent opponents of the gospel, not so much for his own sake, but for the sake of the financial offering he was collecting from Gentile churches to give to the church at Jerusalem (Rom. 15:31). A similar prayer request for deliverance from wicked men is to be found in 2 Thessalonians 3:1–2, "that the message of the Lord may spread rapidly and be honoured".

God is interested and involved in every aspect of our lives, and he longs to reassure us of that, if only we will bring it all to him. Conversely, we will find our minds and hearts to be most in tune with God's purposes when, in prayer, every aspect of our lives is directed towards his glory.

*Dear Father God, I praise you that you know my life intimately. I give all my anxieties to you. May I know your peace. I thank you that you are sovereign over all that happens in your world. Please guard the hearts and minds of your people who are overcome by turmoil or opposition, for the sake of your glory. Amen.*

# DAY 21: PRAYER FOR THE SPREAD OF THE GOSPEL

> Always keep on praying for all God's people. Pray also for me, that whenever I speak, words may be given me so that I will fearlessly make known the mystery of the gospel, for which I am an ambassador in chains.
>
> Ephesians 6:18–20

Most of all, Paul covets prayer for the spread of the gospel. Supremely, his missionary concern is for his own nation, the Jewish people: "Brothers and sisters, my heart's desire and prayer to God for the Israelites is that they may be saved" (Rom. 10:1).

This is very different from many a modern churchgoer who is dubious about the propriety of evangelism in the first place, and of evangelising men and women of other faiths in particular. After all, we live in a pluralist society. The Roman Empire was far more pluralist, however, and it was in that pluralist Roman Empire that the gospel of Christ rang out loud, clear and distinct. Paul's prayer was that its message might be even more clear and powerful, and his example underlined that prayer. Whether in Jewish or Gentile country, whether in prison or at large, this amazing man had a surpassing passion – to make Jesus known. Towards the end of his life we find his astonishing claim: "From Jerusalem all the way around to Illyricum, I have fully proclaimed the gospel of Christ. It has always been my ambition to preach the gospel where Christ was not known" (Rom. 15:19–20). When he is writing to the Philippians from prison, he tells of the way his guards are hearing the gospel from his lips (Phil. 1:13) and almost his last charge to his younger colleague, Timothy, is "Preach the word; be prepared in season and out of season" (2 Tim. 4:2).

Wanted: Christians who are fearless in their witness to Jesus.

*Everlasting Lord, I thank you for the witness of evangelists like Paul, through whom your word has spread throughout the world. Please give courage to all those who strive to make the gospel known. May I never be ashamed to speak out your glorious truth. Amen.*

# DAY 22: PRAYER THAT IS WELL INFORMED

In all my prayers for all of you, I always pray with joy because of your partnership in the gospel from the first day until now ... I am amply supplied, now that I have received from Epaphroditus the gifts you sent ... And my God will meet all your needs according to the riches of his glory in Christ Jesus.

Philippians 1:4–5; 4:18–19

When Epaphroditus brings Paul news of the church in Philippi, together with a gift from them, Paul's excitement is as unmistakable as the information with which his prayers are tinged. Even in a spiritually mixed situation like Corinth, we find Paul thanking God for the believers' gifts, and for the grace of God so evident among them. He is able then to write to them with knowledge and to pray for them with confidence. You can imagine him squeezing every drop of local information from the visitors who brought him news (1 Cor. 1:11).

It is exactly the same story with the Colossians. Paul's prayers for them are stimulated when information about their turning to God arrives via Epaphras, one of their number who came to visit the apostle: "We always thank God ... because we have heard of your faith in Christ Jesus and of the love you have for all God's people ... For this reason ... we have not stopped praying for you" (Col. 1:3, 4, 9).

The undercurrent of prayer for particular churches is one of the lovely minor keys in the Epistles: "I thank my God ... because your faith is being reported all over the world ... I remember you in my prayers at all times" (Rom. 1:8–10). We find the same informed prayer and vivid memory operating for individuals too (Philem. v. 4; 2 Tim. 1:3). Armed with this information, the apostle goes to prayer.

It is not the length of our prayers that matters, but the intention: bringing people or congregations to mind in the presence of the Lord.

> *Gracious Lord, I thank you for those I know who are at the outset of their Christian journey. I think of their circumstances, the challenges they face, their excitement about the gospel – and ask that you will continue to meet all their needs. Please give me a lasting love and concern for them. Amen.*

# *The Nature of Paul's Prayers*

## DAY 23: PRAYER PROMPTED BY THE SPIRIT

> The Spirit helps us in our weakness. We do not know what
> we ought to pray for, but the Spirit himself intercedes for us
> through wordless groans. And he who searches our hearts
> knows the mind of the Spirit, because the Spirit intercedes for
> God's people in accordance with the will of God.
>
> Romans 8:26–27

It was when Paul was allowing the Spirit to prompt prayers within him that he was most confident of a positive answer. He has already made it plain that one of the surest marks of being a Christian is the presence of the Holy Spirit in our hearts, enabling us to look up to God and call him "*Abba,* Daddy" (see Rom. 8:15). The Holy Spirit is the member of the Godhead who resides within the heart of the believer.

When the Spirit prompts prayers within us and we turn to the Father with them in the name of Jesus, we can be confident that the Father knows what is in the mind of the Spirit and will answer positively. This is a strongly trinitarian understanding of prayer. It is a great encouragement for us to wait on God and allow his Spirit, like a spring in the ground of our hearts, to bubble up with the matters for which we should be praying. Deep calls to deep when the Father hears and interprets the groanings of the Spirit on our behalf. Indeed, a possible translation of Romans 8:28 is rooted in this same thought: "The Spirit pleads for God's own people in God's own way, and in everything he cooperates for good with those who are called by God's purpose."

*Loving Father, please still my heart and allow your Spirit to stir the deepest part of my being. May he prompt my prayers and speak for me when my words are too limited, according to your will. Amen.*

# Day 24: Acute battles in prayer

For though we live in the world, we do not wage war as the world does. The weapons we fight with are not the weapons of the world. On the contrary, they have divine power to demolish strongholds.

2 Corinthians 10:3–4

*P*aul and his friends knew times when there was an acute battle in prayer. He calls it "agonising" prayer in Colossians: "Epaphras ... is always wrestling in prayer for you" (Col. 4:12). It is the Greek word used in Jesus' prayer in the Garden: "Being in anguish, he prayed more earnestly, and his sweat was like drops of blood falling to the ground" (Luke 22:44). Paul knew that there was a great outside hindrance to our prayers – Satan. He knew that human effort alone counted for little, but that prayer counted for much.

The modern church in the West knows little of direct prayer against the forces of darkness, but there are signs that, as the fascination of the occult and overt Satanism increase, some Christians are beginning to awaken to the importance of spiritual warfare through prayer and fasting. Certainly, in our own lives, direct prayer against Satan in our personal spiritual battles is enormously effective.

There is no doubt that this figured significantly in Paul's many-sided understanding of prayer. It is therefore with no exaggeration that he can advise his friends in Thessalonica, "Pray continually" (1 Thess. 5:17). This is what he had learned to do. Prayer without leaving long gaps *(adialeiptōs)* is one of the great secrets of successful Christian living. Indeed, no Christian living can be fruitful without it.

*Almighty Lord, I bring to you the battles of my life and ask you to rid Satan from them. Allow him no hold in the hearts of those who seek you, I pray, that we might be more than conquerors for your gospel and your kingdom. Amen.*

# DAY 25: PRAYERS OF QUIET ADORATION

> I kneel before the Father ... I pray that you ... may have
> power, together with all God's people, to grasp how wide and
> long and high and deep is the love of Christ, and to know this
> love that surpasses knowledge – that you may be filled to the
> measure of all the fulness of God.
>
> Ephesians 3:14, 17–19

At times, prayer is a matter of remembering people and needs before the Lord. At times it is a gentle resting in God and his abundant love, a profound openness to him without words or petitions.

In his letter to the Ephesians, we join Paul in his deep contemplation of the living God. It is a profoundly moving picture of Paul, the man of prayer, on his knees before his heavenly Father, simply weighed down with amazement at the enormity of the love of this God who has deigned to allow Christ's Spirit to come and dwell in his heart in response to his cry of faith. In such contemplation the human spirit is taken beyond itself and deeply nourished.

It is in the attitude of quiet adoration and awe that God is most readily able to communicate with his people. Tears may wet one person's eyes; another may make an encouraging prophetic utterance. It is simply the Lord breaking gently in upon his people who are turned to him in quiet expectation.

*Living God, I am amazed by your infinite love, which has given everything for me. I hardly have the words to express my gratitude to you. Please continue to nourish my spirit according to your will. Amen.*

# DAY 26: PRAYERS OF EXULTANT PRAISE

Praise be to the God and Father of our Lord Jesus Christ, who
has blessed us in the heavenly realms with every spiritual blessing in Christ.

Ephesians 1:3

Paul's prayer is also marked by exultant praise. He will break
his sequence of thought simply in order to burst out in an
expression of praise: "Now to the King eternal, immortal, invisible, the only God, be honour and glory for ever and ever. Amen"
(1 Tim. 1:17).

I love that instinctive apostrophe or pause, that lifting of the
eyes to say to God, "You are wonderful." Many of the deepest
moments in my own prayer life are prompted by occasions when
I do just that – drop everything and simply turn to God in short
but heartfelt praise. It is what Brother Lawrence would call "prac-
tising the presence of Christ".

*Lord Jesus, Heavenly King, I praise you for all that you are
throughout eternity and for all that you have done for your people.
Please fix my gaze on you, now and always. Amen.*

# DAY 27: A PRAYER FOR ONESIPHORUS

May the Lord show mercy to the household of Onesiphorus,
because he often refreshed me and was not ashamed of my
chains. On the contrary, when he was in Rome, he searched
hard for me until he found me. May the Lord grant that he
will find mercy from the Lord on that day! You know very well
in how many ways he helped me in Ephesus.

2 Timothy 1:16–18

How we would love to know a bit more about Onesiphorus! The New Testament is silent, but a mid-second-
century work, *The Acts of Paul and Thecla,* says he was a citizen
of Iconium who, along with his wife Lectra, entertained Paul on
his first missionary journey and was converted through him. At
all events, he had a household and a residence in Ephesus and,
like many of the wealthy merchants of the day, made occasional
visits to Rome. On one of them he heard of Paul's imprisonment
and made diligent efforts to track him down. What a lot it must
have meant to Paul to receive a visit like that from a trusted
friend. Prison can be not only lonely but also very dispiriting.

Paul is still basking in the joy and encouragement of Onesiphorus's visit as he writes to Timothy at Ephesus. He wants to
show his gratitude for the visit by praying God's richest blessing
upon the household from which it came. Here is an important
example of praying for the whole social milieu of a particular person. We are all influenced greatly by our family situation, and it
is good to know that friends who love us are praying about that.

Onesiphorus is not forgotten; far from it. But instead of simply lifting him to God in gratitude, Paul does something much
more important. He prays that Onesiphorus's whole lifestyle may

be so Christlike that when he, in turn, comes to face death (Paul was at this point very much contemplating his own death – see 2 Tim. 4:6ff) he will be able to look up confidently to the Lord for his mercy. "Mercy" and "the day" are prominent in this letter. It would be good if we pleasure-loving, complacent, twenty-first-century Christians took both more seriously. One day we shall die, and then above all else we shall stand in need of the sheer unmerited mercy of the Lord. How wonderful when a Christian friend, like Paul, has the insight and directness to pray for just that.

> *Heavenly Father, I thank you for those Christians who have been faithful to me and my loved ones in prayer. May I too learn to lift my friends and fellow Christians to you, so that they may continue in the faith until the day of your return. Amen.*

# PART 3

# Prayer for Christians Paul Knew Well

# *Praying for the Philippians*

## DAY 28: PAUL'S FONDNESS FOR PHILIPPI

> Paul and Timothy, servants of Christ Jesus, To all the saints in Christ Jesus at Philippi, together with the overseers and deacons: Grace and peace to you from God our Father and the Lord Jesus Christ.
>
> Philippians 1:1–2

Philippi! How the apostle Paul thrilled to that name. It meant a great deal in the course of his ministry, for it had been to Philippi that he had gone when he received a vision of the man from Macedonia beckoning him over into Europe. Philippi was one of the foremost cities in the great Roman province of Macedonia, which comprised the whole of Northern Greece. It was a tough nut to crack since it was founded as a Roman colony and was full of retired soldiers from the legions. Nonetheless, it was here that Paul managed to plant a tiny church, inaugurated at the Jewish meeting place for prayer by the river.

We know of three of its first members. One was Lydia, a leading businesswoman. One was a slave girl who had been deeply into the occult and had been set free through Paul's ministry. The third was the gaoler of the prison into which Paul had been thrown for preaching the gospel. It was hardly a promising beginning, but the church grew and prospered, possibly under the guidance and pastoral care of Luke. A few years later, when the letter to the Philippians was written, it had clearly become a force to be reckoned with, complete with its own bishops and deacons, and its own dynamic and generous – if occasionally disruptive – church life.

So it is no surprise that Paul is full of warmth as he sets about writing to this church that he evangelised ten years earlier. Once again he is in prison, and it appears that they have just sent him a gift of money, and probably provisions, through one of their number, Epaphroditus (Phil. 2:25ff). He writes to thank them and to deal with a number of other issues – but first and foremost we find him at prayer for them.

*Gracious Lord, I thank you for Paul's example in evangelism and in prayer for his converts. I pray that you will give me a passion for helping others to know you and to grow in you. Amen.*

# Paul's Approach to Prayer

## DAY 29: REGULAR PRAYER WITH JOYFUL THANKSGIVING

I thank my God every time I remember you. In all my prayers for all of you, I always pray with joy because of your partnership in the gospel from the first day until now.

Philippians 1:3–5

Not surprisingly, Paul's approach to prayer follows a similar pattern in his various letters. Once we have formed good habits in prayer, they tend to serve us well.

His prayer was *regular*. He may not have prayed at length each time he remembered them, but recall them he did, turning recollection into prayer. It is striking how many times phrases like "making mention of you in my prayers" come in the New Testament. They point to Christians who were living so close to God that memory flowed naturally into prayer.

His prayer was *thankful*. It would be wonderful if gratitude could be picked out as a major strand in our prayer life. All too often we are insistent in asking, but forgetful of the need to come back and thank God for what he has done. Paul did not make that mistake. Thankfulness marks his prayers; it is a hallmark of authentic spirituality.

His prayer was *joyful*. Often prayer seems a drudgery, a duty, joyless. In corporate prayer, requests are a solemn rigmarole rather than joyful interaction with a generous God. Joy was one of the most notable characteristics of Jesus: that is what drew people to him. He was so radiantly alive. And he promised that his joy would remain as a gift to his followers (John 15:11). Alas, it is a gift that many have never unpacked.

His prayer was *reflective*. As Paul prayed, he must have given himself time to reflect on all that had taken place "from the first day until now". What memories must have flooded into his mind! The eight-mile tramp down the Via Egnatia from the port of Neapolis to the open-air prayer place. Lydia, "whose heart the Lord opened" – *Lord, please keep her heart open to you,* he might have prayed. The slave girl – *Lord, do not allow those evil forces to come back and dominate her life; protect her, Lord Jesus.* The magistrates who had thrown him and Silas into prison – *Lord, get through to them in your own time and your own way.* And the gaoler – *Lord, thank you so much for him!* As he reflected on people and events there, it is little wonder that memory led Paul into thanksgiving for the church at Philippi, their conversion, their growth, their care for him, their zeal in evangelism.

> *Loving Father, I praise you that you have made me spiritually alive. Teach me to live close to you in prayer, in joyful gratitude for all that you have done in my life and in the lives of those I know and love. Amen.*

# DAY 30: INSPIRED BY AFFINITY IN THE GOSPEL

> Because of your partnership in the gospel ... whether I am in
> chains or defending and confirming the gospel, all of you share
> in God's grace with me.
>
> Philippians 1:5, 7

*W*hy did Paul give so much time and care to intercession for his friends and their churches? It is, after all, very
hard work to sustain week after week, year after year.

Twice in rapid succession, Paul uses the key Christian word
for fellowship, *koinōnia*. It lurks under the English words translated "partnership" and "partakers". It means joint participation,
sharing in something together. So what did this mercurial apostle share in common with the retired sergeant majors at Philippi?

They shared *a common gospel* (v. 5): the same good news of
Jesus the Saviour and the Lord which had brought this proud
Pharisee to his knees had penetrated the Roman colony in
Philippi. The gospel had made new people of them all. This is a
powerful inducement to prayer, especially prayer for those we
have led to faith. Because we share this same mighty instrument
of God's good news, we can pray with joy and confidence for one
another.

They also shared *a common task* (v. 7): the defence and con-
firmation of the gospel. Peter uses the same Greek word,
"defence", when he encourages his readers, "Always be prepared
to make a defence to any one who calls you to account for the
hope that is in you" (1 Pet. 3:15, RSV). There are good reasons for
the Christian faith and we need to know what we believe and why,
being prepared to say so confidently. Paul's other word, "confir-
mation", speaks of the competent nurture of young Christians, of

training Christian workers. Paul and his converts at Philippi were involved together in this ministry of apologetics and nurture. It is a powerful platform on which to build reciprocal prayer, as both parties know the joys and difficulties of the task to which they are committed.

Paul also reminds them that they share *a common grace* (v. 7). Here "grace" means strength. We, and those for whom we pray, are all equally recipients of the Lord's gracious strength for our daily battles – if we ask him. The same Lord who sustains us will sustain them as we pray for them. And that is a good ground for prayer, if ever there was one.

Sharing helps praying.

*All-powerful Lord, I thank you for the life and purpose that the gospel gives to Christians everywhere. I thank you that you give us your strength for the challenges we face. Help me to remember this in my life and as I bring before you the needs of my brothers and sisters in Christ. Amen.*

# DAY 31: INSPIRED BY ASSURANCE OF GOD'S WILL

> Being confident of this, that he who began a good work in
> you will carry it on to completion until the day of Christ Jesus
> ... I have you in my heart ... God can testify how I long for
> all of you with the affection of Christ Jesus.
>
> Philippians 1:6–8

The Philippians' perseverance these ten years had proved the reality of God's work in them. His love would not let them go. Their survival and growth was guaranteed by the nature of God himself, the utterly consistent one.

Paul may have been brooding recently on Psalm 138, with its wonderful words,

> Though I walk in the midst of trouble,
>     you preserve my life;
> you stretch out your hand against the anger of my foes,
>     with your right hand you save me.
> The LORD will fulfil his purpose for me;
>     your love, O LORD, endures for ever –
>     do not abandon the works of your hands.
>
> vv. 7–8

He who has begun will complete. What a picture that conjures up of the one who is both Alpha and Omega. He holds in his mighty hands both the prisoner at Rome and the congregation at Philippi. He will complete the tapestry of their lives which he has begun to weave. There is no doubt whatever about his will and his power in this matter, and so Paul prays with deep assurance. Knowing God's will helps our prayer.

Paul also seems to have a mixture of natural affection for these bluff northerners, combined with the *agapē* love derived from the heart of Jesus himself. Natural affection is often a guide that indicates for whom we should be praying. Supernatural love is the fire which keeps it burning. Today we prize love, and despise prayer. In those days, if you loved, you prayed. In Paul we see a man who lived so close to Jesus Christ that he loved with Christ's affection as well as with his own natural bonds of friendship.

Loving helps prayer.

*Everlasting God, I stand in awe at your purposes for believers throughout history, in the present day, and on into eternity. May your unchanging faithfulness inspire my loving prayer for my Christian friends and acquaintances. Amen.*

# Paul's Requests in Prayer

## DAY 32: PRAYER FOR ABUNDANT LOVE

And this is my prayer: that your love may abound more and
more.

Philippians 1:9

Paul's prayer for the Philippians majors on two great themes,
love and fruitfulness, and he develops each one as he medi-
tates and pours out his prayer to God.

Love is the number one priority – not sentiment, not liking,
not desire, but true love. Love, *agapē,* means the outgoing of the
whole personality in sacrificial service. God's love is like that. He
did not feel sentimental about the world, did not like it, did not
have any stirrings of lust about it; no, he loved it. That is why he
sent his beloved Son to die and rise for us, so that we could be set
free to respond to such undreamed-of generosity. No wonder the
early Christians practically invented the word *agapē,* to denote
such love. There was nothing like it in the ancient world. *Agapē*
means the joining of our heart to the object of our love, and the
devotion of our life to his or her good. God is like that in his love,
and it is the supreme mark of the Master in the disciple. It is the
clinching evidence that our Christian profession is real. That is
why Paul prays for love in the Philippian church. It is the bench-
mark of belonging.

He prays for *abundant love*. Paul thinks perhaps of a great river breaking its banks and flooding the meadows alongside. He longs to see in the Philippians a Christian love which reaches out not to some, but to all; not occasionally, but habitually; not in talk, but in action. We do not manage to produce love like this. It needs constant replenishing from the spring in the heart of God himself.

He also prays for *increasing love*. Progress is an essential part of life. It certainly is in Christian discipleship. You cannot remain stationary as a Christian, any more than you can remain stationary on a bicycle. Love is the language of the Godhead. It is impossible to have too much of it; our progress in the Christian life is marked by progress in love above all else. Nor is such love an emotional thing. It has a cognitive aspect and a practical outworking, as Paul makes plain in the unfolding of his prayer.

> *Dear Lord and Saviour, I praise you for your sacrificial love for the world. I pray that this love may flow into the hearts of those in my church community, and be the mark of my life. Amen.*

# DAY 33: PRAYER FOR A DEEP KNOWLEDGE OF CHRIST

And this is my prayer: that your love may abound more and more in knowledge and depth of insight, so that you may be able to discern what is best.

Philippians 1:9–10

*L*ove and knowledge are not foes, but friends. So Paul prays that the Philippians' love will produce a deeper knowledge of Christ. The word used for "knowledge" here, *epignōsis,* does not mean academic competence: it means knowledge of Jesus in a profound, personal way. The love which has been deepened by growing knowledge of Jesus will gradually develop discernment. If we have learned to love Jesus we shall become better at discerning him under the cloak of daily events, and will find a growing discrimination in our lives for him, desiring to seek out his pleasure. The Greek here could mean that you "discriminate between things that differ": we need that discrimination in this confusing world. It could also mean that you "approve things that are excellent". Genuine discrimination leads the believer to make sound decisions, always seeking God's best for any situation.

There is a deep inner logic to this prayer. If a love is growing in us to produce discriminating knowledge, we shall be ready to meet the Lord at the "day of Christ". This day may be when we die, or it may be that we shall be part of the generation which sees Jesus' return. In either case it will be decisive. If, though we cannot see him, we have learned to discern him and please him among ordinary events and ordinary challenges from ordinary people, we shall all the more readily recognise him on that day.

*Lord Jesus, as I grow in my knowledge and love of you, my focus is sharpened on your involvement in my life and in the world. I ask that I, and those whom I hold dearest, may always seek your will in all that we do, in preparation for eternity. Amen.*

# DAY 34: PRAYING FOR PURE AND BLAMELESS LIVING

> And this is my prayer: that your love may abound more and
> more in knowledge and depth of insight, so that you may be
> able to discern what is best and may be pure and blameless for
> the day of Christ.
>
> Philippians 1:9–10

*I*n preparation for the day when we will meet Christ, we are also called to be pure and blameless, to work out lovingly the righteousness with which Jesus generously invests us when we begin to follow him.

So Paul prays that the Philippians' motives will be "pure". The word here, *eilikrinēs*, means "sincere", or "judged in the light of the sun". Interestingly, both translations take us back to the ancient practice of beekeeping: honey needed to be "sincere" (Latin "without wax"), and that was judged by holding the honey up to the light of the sun to see if there were particles of wax in the product. A beautiful image! Paul longs for their motives to be as pure as refined honey. And that happens when, in any uncertain matter, we give the Lord the benefit of the doubt and trust in him.

Paul is also concerned about the Philippians' actions. If they are to be blameless, *aproskopoi,* they will be "not stumbling blocks". Our lives are meant to be stepping stones, not stumbling blocks, to Christ. That word, "not stumbling blocks", can be taken in an active or passive sense, meaning either "giving no offence" or "taking no offence". They fit together. We shall not be able to face Christ with equanimity on that day if our actions have caused God's little ones to stumble (2 Cor. 5:10). We, too, face judgment.

> *Righteous Lord, my life seems so very far from the purity to which you call us. Please refine my thoughts and actions, so that I may be a true witness to those who would follow you. Amen.*

# DAY 35: PRAYER FOR THE FRUIT OF OUTREACH

> And this is my prayer: that your love may abound more and more in knowledge and depth of insight, so that you may be able to discern what is best and may be pure and blameless for the day of Christ, filled with the fruit of righteousness that comes through Jesus Christ.
>
> Philippians 1:9–11

If love in all its depth is one great concern of the apostle for his converts, fruitfulness is the other. An unfruitful life is an insult to God and unattractive to men and women. God is like a gardener who comes seeking fruit. And when he finds lives like the barren fig trees in the Gospels, they call down his righteous judgment, his curse.

Alongside the fruit of holy lives, pure motives and practical goodness, Paul longed to see the fruit of outreach in the Philippians. It is clear that they were trying to do this, but some were preaching Christ "out of envy" for Paul and "selfish ambition", while others were doing it "out of goodwill" and "love" (Phil. 1:15ff). Still, they did it, and for that Paul rejoiced. Paul was not looking for clones of himself, but for disciples of Jesus.

Paul's example of outreach in prison gave the Philippians confidence, and enabled the good news to spread throughout the Praetorian Guard, the crack troops of the Roman Empire, one of whose duties was to guard significant prisoners (vv. 12–14). Bars and shackles could not keep Paul from spreading the gospel. It was his lifeblood; and it was effective. At the end of this letter, God's people with Paul send the Philippians their greetings, "especially those who belong to Caesar's household" (Phil. 4:22). How fruitful the gospel had been on his lips!

Outreach is the lifeblood of Christianity. It is nothing to do with personality or denomination. God expects this twofold fruit, holy living and outward looking, from all of us. And, praise be, he enables us to find it "through Jesus Christ". But how easily we lose heart! We must pray for others on this score, as Paul did from his prison cell. And we must ask others to pray for us in this matter too.

> *Loving Father, please fill my church with the lifeblood of your gospel, so that we may have the energy and confidence of Paul to reach others for you, for the sake of your glory. Amen.*

# Paul's Goal in Prayer

## DAY 36: COOPERATING WITH GOD IN PRAYER

And this is my prayer: that your love may abound more and
more in knowledge and depth of insight, so that you may be
able to discern what is best and may be pure and blameless for
the day of Christ, filled with the fruit of righteousness that
comes through Jesus Christ – to the glory and praise of God.

Philippians 1:9–11

The concluding words of this great prayer are important.
Paul cherishes no illusion of empire-building at Philippi for
his own sake. Nor is he praying solely for the sake of his friends
there. What he most longs for is God's glory!

He wants the glory of God to shine out like a beacon, so that
all can see it and be attracted to it. And there, in this Roman
colony, full of battle-hardened warriors, men and women will see
God's glory as Paul himself has, and adore him for all that he is.

Paul is looking, in the long run, for nothing less than a creation back in touch with its Creator, a world where God's will
shall be done on earth as it is in heaven. That is how the Master
taught us to pray. Should disciples not make it their supreme goal

perate in a small way through their prayers with the Cre-
s grand, cosmic design?

*Creator God, I praise you for the lives of those through whom your glory shines, and ask that I, and my Christian family, may be in touch with you and your will so that we may serve you in your grand design. Amen.*

# DAY 37: A PRAYER FOR ALEXANDER

> Alexander the metalworker did me a great deal of harm. The
> Lord will repay him for what he has done. You too should be
> on your guard against him, because he strongly opposed our
> message. At my first defence, no-one came to my support, but
> everyone deserted me. May it not be held against them. But
> the Lord stood at my side and gave me strength, so that
> through me the message might be fully proclaimed and all the
> Gentiles might hear it. And I was delivered from the lion's
> mouth. The Lord will rescue me from every evil attack and
> will bring me safely to his heavenly kingdom. To him be glory
> for ever and ever. Amen.
>
> 2 Timothy 4:14–18

These sentences are more of a statement than a prayer,
and yet they are shaped in a similar structure to Paul's
prayers, working through several ideas about God and ending
with wholehearted praise. They might also help us in our prayers
when we are facing opposition and hardship.

What Alexander did to harm Paul we may never know. In all
probability he was a leader in one of the metalworking guilds who
were so angered by Paul's preaching against idolatry, and therefore
against their business. We find that kind of feeling exploding at
Ephesus a few years earlier in the famous scene sketched so bril-
liantly by Luke in Acts 19. At all events, Paul had found this
Alexander a very dangerous opponent.

Some of the manuscripts read, "May the Lord repay him
according to his deeds." But the better manuscripts make it a
solemn statement of fact: "The Lord will repay him." We can
leave vengeance to the Lord because he will repay, at his time, in

way, with his justice (Rom. 12:19). So here is not, in all probability, a prayer for retribution, but a statement of the awesome fact that God will judge one day, and we can safely leave our wrongs with the one who is incorruptible Justice and perfect Love.

Paul's own forgiving attitude to those who have forsaken him is clearly seen in verse 16: "May it not be held against them." Such an attitude lifts his mind out of a lonely and unjust situation to focus on Christ's faithfulness and purpose, "so that through me the message might be fully proclaimed". Assured of his past, present and future security in Christ, he gives all praise to God.

> *Forgiving Lord, may I be gracious to those who have wronged me, conscious of your mercy towards me. Let me rest assured that in your perfect justice you will deal with those who have harmed me, so that I will not feel alone or abandoned, but safe in the steadfast security you give. Amen.*

PART 4

# Prayer for the Mission Field

# *Praying for the Colossians*

## DAY 38: PAUL'S CONCERN FOR COLOSSAE

I want you to know how hard I am contending for you and for
those at Laodicea, and for all who have not met me personally.

Colossians 2:1

*Most* of us find prayer for missionary work very difficult. It is so hard to project ourselves into a foreign country, with a different language, different customs and different
lifestyles. How should we pray for such people? How should we
pray for those who have left our country to spread the gospel
overseas? All too often, in our prayers for Christians we have
never met, in lands we do not know, we resort to vague, blanket
prayers: "Lord, bless them anyway." It was not like that with the
apostle Paul.

He is writing from prison, probably in Rome. He has a small
group of Christian friends around him, who apparently are free
to go where they please. And he sends two of them to a church he
has never seen, the Christian community at Colossae, a town sit-
uated in the Lycus Valley, on the main road from Ephesus to the
East. We do not know when Colossae began to respond to the
gospel of Christ, but it was probably in the mid-fifties of the first
century when Paul was at the height of his influence at Ephesus,

speaking boldly and persuasively on a daily basis about the good news of Jesus. We are told, "This went on for two years, so that all the Jews and Greeks who lived in the province of Asia heard the word of the Lord" (Acts 19:10).

One of Paul's friends, Epaphras, clearly played a leading part in church-planting there, and it was he who brought to the apostle the news about the Colossian church which sparked this letter (Col. 4:12). Paul longed to meet the Christians there, and his prayer for them is a prime example of the way he interceded powerfully and imaginatively for missions and for fellow believers who were utter strangers to him.

> *Almighty Lord, I thank you for the way that you used Paul to begin your worldwide mission, and for his faithfulness in prayer for the churches he had never met. Please show me how to pray meaningfully for fellow Christians and missionaries around the world, for the sake of your gospel. Amen.*

# The Characteristics of Paul's Prayer

## DAY 39: PERSISTENT PRAYER

> Since the day we heard about you, we have not stopped praying for you. We continually ask God . . .
>
> Colossians 1:9

A number of things stand out as we read a prayer like this and try to put ourselves in Paul's shoes as he lies there in prison. His prayer was immediate. As soon as he heard the news from Epaphras, he prayed. Here is a man who turns news items into prayer. He does not wait until his evening devotions. He prays then and there.

His prayer was informed. You can imagine him chatting enthusiastically with Epaphras, anxious to glean all the information he could about this exciting new church which nevertheless betrayed dangerous tendencies. If our prayers are to be effective, especially for those we do not know, it is important to be informed. In this respect, videos, missionary prayer diaries and personal friendships with those who know the place for which we are praying are all invaluable.

His prayer was persistent. On and on he prayed. He did not pray once and then forget about it. He steadily set himself to intercede. God has his own reasons for delaying a reply to our prayers. Sometimes it is to test our sincerity, to see if we really desire what we have prayed for.

His prayer was loving – at least, that is what the words "praying" and "asking" suggest to me. He meant business, because he cared about them. True prayer is the overflow of love towards both God and man.

His prayer was corporate. He had clearly gathered Epaphras, Onesimus, Tychicus and Aristarchus together for prayer about the situation at Colossae (Col. 4:7ff). It would have been great to have been a fly on the wall at those prayer meetings. The unity of spirit, the earnestness, the love would have taught us so much. Prayer does not need to be either solitary or confined to liturgical settings. These prayers were held corporately, informally and no doubt very uncomfortably on the floor of a Roman prison!

*Dear Father God, I pray that you will bring into my path those around the world for whom you would have me pray. I ask that you will give me a passion for their cultures and a deep love for their churches. Teach me with my Christian friends to intercede persistently for them, so that we may see your faithfulness to them and us at work. Amen.*

# DAY 40: GRATEFUL AND COSTLY PRAYER

> We always thank God, the Father of our Lord Jesus Christ,
> when we pray for you, because we have heard of your faith . . .
> and love . . . [and] hope.
>
> Colossians 1:3–5

*P*aul's prayer for the Colossians is *grateful*. He expresses heartfelt gratitude to God that they have entrusted their lives to Christ and are beginning to manifest his love, and that the gospel is "bearing fruit and growing" among them (v. 6).

At the same time, his prayer is *unselfish*. He did not dump his own problems on the Colossians, great though these were. He was lonely, cold, hungry, imprisoned and unable to pursue his vocation. But he was entirely concerned for them, their welfare and their growth. If we pay too much attention to our own concerns we will never grow in maturity and sympathy: we will come to think that the world centres on ourselves, and we will shrivel in consequence.

Further, Paul's prayer is *costly*. When he speaks in 2:1 about "how hard I am contending for you", he uses a powerful word, *agōn,* meaning literally a battle or wrestling match. It is the word used of Jesus praying with intense passion in the Garden of Gethsemane. Prayer is hard work. It is hard not only because we are lazy, weak and forgetful, but also because there is great external hindrance to prayer. Satan is a reality. There is a war on. Prayer keeps the communication lines open with God, the only source of our strength, and for that very reason it will be relentlessly attacked by the enemy of souls. If he can isolate us from God, he has us at his mercy.

We need to wake up to the vital importance of determined prayer which confronts the powers of darkness (cf. Eph. 6:10–20), loosening their unseen grip on circumstances and people. Alien though this is to our sceptical, secularised minds, prayer involves spiritual battle. Those who are most willing to enter into the battle are those who most frequently see their prayers answered.

> *Gracious Father, I thank you for the amazing growth of churches around the world, often in the face of persecution. Please watch over my Christian brothers and sisters far away from here and bring them to maturity in you, so that as we pray for one another the might of your hand will be seen across the globe. Amen.*

# The Contents of Paul's Prayer

## DAY 41: PRAYER FOR THE UNDERSTANDING OF GOD'S WILL

> We continually ask God to fill you with the knowledge of his will through all the wisdom and understanding that the Spirit gives.
>
> Colossians 1:9

It is fascinating to overhear Paul at prayer for this church of strangers. It was not "God bless the Colossians", or "We remember before you the church at Colossae", but powerful and specific intercession. And this is how he did it: he prayed for knowledge, obedience and strength.

Nothing could be more important for the Christian than knowing God's will. It was the keynote of Jesus' life: "I always do what pleases him", he said of his relationship with his heavenly Father (John 8:29). As he faced the appalling destiny of the cross, and naturally shrank from it, he prayed, "yet not my will, but yours be done" (Luke 22:42). And he taught his disciples to pray, "your will be done on earth as it is in heaven" (Matt. 6:10). That should be the goal of our lives.

And yet it is so difficult. We wish we knew what God's will was on this or that matter. We wish we could read it off instantaneously like the results from an internet search. We all know it is not like that. But the question of God's will is not all that obscure either. A great deal of his will is made known to us in the Bible – more than enough to live by.

As we, and those we pray for, study the Bible on a regular basis, we will have a growing awareness of God's will. It makes sense to pray that those who have come to faith may realise the purposes for which God has called them, and may be able to discern his will for their lives. Knowledge is not to be shunned, but welcomed, as long as it issues not in arrogance but in obedience. Indeed, full knowledge is the greatest safeguard against error.

Christian wisdom *(sophia)* and Christian shrewdness of perception *(sunesis)* are two of the choicest blessings God can bestow. This overall understanding of his will, this occasional flash of insight into his purposes, generally comes through patient daily study of the Word of God and a willingness to follow it. That is the sort of person to whom God can disclose his will. To pray for this knowledge through wisdom and understanding is one of the greatest things we can do for others, whether we have met them or not.

*Dear Lord, I find it so difficult to be patient, waiting on your will. Please give me the desire and discipline to read your Word regularly so that I may learn of your purposes. I ask that you will give Christians in this country and abroad a real understanding of your will, so that they will walk faithfully with you. Amen.*

# DAY 42: PRAYER FOR OBEDIENCE TO GOD'S WILL

> We continually ask God to fill you with the knowledge of his will . . . so that you may live a life worthy of the Lord and please him in every way.
>
> Colossians 1:9–10

Knowledge is never an end in itself. It is meant to lead to obedience. God does not reveal to us many things we would love to know; rather, he shows us enough light to walk by. He does not commit himself to answering our speculative questions: "Why should suffering occur?" or "What becomes of those who have not heard the gospel?" He simply expects his truth to be obeyed. It is his responsibility to reveal his will to us; it is our responsibility to obey it. Paul wants the Colossians to know God's purpose for their lives, and he wants them to achieve it. He sums up in a succinct sentence the life of the person who obeys God's will.

It will be a *consistent* life, worthy of the Lord, a life that is a credit to Jesus Christ. If church people lived like that, there would be an infinitely greater hunger in society to know the reason why! What a way to pray for others: that they may lead lives that are worthy of Jesus.

It will also be a *sensitive* life, fully pleasing to him. Here is a marvellous touchstone of authentic Christian ethics. They do not consist of slavish obedience to some rule book, but of loving devotion to a person. It is significant that the New Testament is very short on specific ethical injunctions, but this idea of seeking to please Jesus in all we do is central. It is wonderfully flexible: it allows full room for variety in our personalities and perceptions of Jesus. It is wonderfully liberating: not legislation but love relationship. It is wonderfully creative, too: if we really seek to please him in all we do, all manner of new initiatives will emerge. We shall not be bound by the past, but shall be free, as Augustine put it, to "love God – and do what you like". The world needs liberated Christians like that. We do well to pray for them.

> *Loving God, as you light the paths of missionaries and churches across the world, I ask that you will mould your people to respond to your word in loving obedience. May we together live lives worthy of you and truly be free to please you in all that we do. Amen.*

# DAY 43: PRAYER FOR LIVES THAT ABIDE IN CHRIST

> We continually ask God to fill you with the knowledge of his will . . . so that you may live a life worthy of the Lord and please him in every way: bearing fruit in every good work, growing in the knowledge of God.
>
> Colossians 1:9–10

The person who obeys God's will should have a *fruitful* life. "Fruitful" is an evocative word. It conjures up images of trees laden with fruit, fulfilling the purpose of their existence. We need to pray such fruitfulness into being.

Fruit in the New Testament is primarily used to describe the qualities of character which will emerge as we keep in close touch with Christ. "Love, joy, peace, patience, kindness, goodness, faithfulness, gentleness and self-control" – these are the "fruit" or "crop" produced by the Spirit of Jesus indwelling us (Gal. 5:22). Equally, when we help others come to Christ, that is "fruit" or "harvest" – so Paul prays that he may come to Rome to "have a harvest" among them (Rom. 1:13). But neither fruit of character nor of evangelism will be found in us unless we abide in Christ the Vine (see John 15:1–17). Cut off from him, we are just dead branches.

The person obedient to God will also have a *deepening* life, as we saw with the Philippians. How sad it is to see Christians who "died" two or three decades ago, with the same old ideas and prejudices of the past. It is all too possible for people to become spiritually stuck. The water of life in which Christians were spawned gets frozen, and they with it. This is precisely the opposite of what

God wants. He longs for us to grow in our knowledge of him – not just of his will.

In Islam, Allah reveals his will to mortal man, but never his person. That, however, is just what the God revealed in Scripture delights to do. He wants us to know him, in increasing depth and intimacy, as the years go by. How important, then, to pray that this may be true in the lives of those for whom we intercede.

*Heavenly Lord, I praise you for the power of your Spirit to transform us to be fruitful in character and purpose. I pray that you will give life to your churches as they grow richly in their personal knowledge of you. Amen.*

# DAY 44: PRAYER FOR GOD'S
## TRANSFORMING POWER

> We continually ask God to fill you with the knowledge of
> his will . . . so that you may live a life worthy of the Lord . . .
> bearing fruit in every good work . . . being strengthened with
> all power according to his glorious might so that you may
> have great endurance and patience, and giving joyful thanks
> to the Father.
>
> Colossians 1:10–12

Knowledge, obedience, strength: what a trio of spiritual qualities! Paul is well aware that the Lord enables what he commands. He does not ask the impossible of us. One of the most amazing things about God is that he sets us the highest standards, and then offers us the power to at least begin to achieve those standards, slow though the progress is.

Notice, first, the *extent* of this power. It is limitless, "according to his glorious might". This is not some second-rate enabling, but God's glory at work in equipping weak sinners to share that same glory. "Glory" is a deep word in the Bible. In the Old Testament it has the nuance of weight and solidity; in the New Testament it carries the overtones of splendour and light. Both splendour and light, of course, are attributes of God himself. And he has the power to begin the transformation of even such intractable material as ourselves in the direction of glory.

Second, notice the *effect* of this power. It results in "great endurance and patience, and giving joyful thanks". When God's power is welcomed into our hearts it does not make us big-headed, but humble-hearted. It produces not arrogance, but patient endurance with joy – the endurance of prisoners languishing in gaol for the sake of Christ; the patience of missionaries working in situations where they may see little fruit; the joy of people like Mother Teresa who, humanly speaking, had so little to be joyful about. These are the manifestations of the power God wants to instil into his children. Such power changes lives.

These three great requests, for knowledge, obedience and strength, are highly specific, but they are applicable to Christians everywhere, not least to those for whom we are asked to pray but have never met. There is nothing vague about them: they are rooted in God's self-revelation in Scripture. And they are bathed in love, the love with which Paul himself was daily washed by the heavenly Father. We need prayer like that to ricochet around the world.

> *All Powerful God, I praise you for your limitless might to transform us for glory. I pray that the missionaries and persecuted Christians I know of will be strengthened with patience and joy in the hardships they face, that they may know your love. Amen.*

# The Conclusion of Paul's Prayer

## DAY 45: JOYFUL THANKSGIVING

> ... giving joyful thanks to the Father, who has qualified you to share in the inheritance of his people in the kingdom of light. For he has rescued us from the dominion of darkness and brought us into the kingdom of the Son he loves, in whom we have redemption, the forgiveness of sins.
>
> Colossians 1:12–14

Paul ends his prayer just as he began his reflections on these Colossian Christians, with thanksgiving. Clearly it came naturally to him. Thanksgiving before he prays. Thanksgiving afterwards. It is a lovely trait to cultivate. Praise and thanksgiving have many effects. They keep us grateful and remind us of God's greatness and our smallness. They keep us on the lookout for answers to prayer. Thanksgiving as we pray for others enables us to keep mental track of the growth they have been making, and encourages us to further petition. And praise brings a real sense of God's presence and victory to our lives.

Paul thanks God first for the Colossians' *new status*. The Father has qualified them to share in the inheritance of the saints in light. "Saints" is their description: it is applied in the New Testament to all Christians, people who are, literally, "set aside" for him. They used to inhabit the country of darkness. Now that they have come to Christ, they have discovered a totally undreamed-of inheritance. They live in God's country, the Land of Light. They have a totally new spiritual address, a new status, a new citizenship. This is something they can be confident about, for it is God who has qualified them.

Second, Paul thanks God for their *mighty Saviour*. He is robust and decisive in describing the change which their conversion has brought about. Instead of bondage – release. Instead of darkness – light. Instead of alienation from God – the inheritance with the saints. Instead of unbearable guilt – the forgiveness of sins.

What a prayer! What a thanksgiving! And all for people he had never met, as he lay in prison thinking about them and praying for them. Here is a real stimulus to our prayers for missions.

*Mighty Saviour, I give you joyful thanks for my millions of brothers and sisters in Christ around the world. May we together know the forgiveness and freedom of our inheritance, so that we may be set apart for you, living in your kingdom of light. Amen.*

# DAY 46: A PRAYER FOR PHILEMON

> I always thank my God as I remember you in my prayers,
> because I hear about your love for all God's people and your
> faith in the Lord Jesus. I pray that your partnership with us in
> the faith may be effective in deepening your understanding of
> every good thing we share for the sake of Christ.
>
> Philemon 4–6

*P*hilemon was a wealthy landowner living at, or just out-side, Colossae, and Paul wrote to him by the same messenger, Tychicus, who delivered the Colossian letter. Paul had brought Philemon to faith in Jesus some time earlier. Subsequently, one of Philemon's slaves, Onesimus, had run away after stealing a lot of money, and eventually landed up (in the irony of God) in the same prison as Paul. Needless to say, Paul also brings him to Christ, and then together they address the difficult issue of what Onesimus should do to put things right after his release. They decide on a plan unthinkable for those times: Onesimus should go and give himself up, and Philemon should be asked, rather than crucifying this escaped slave as was the normal practice, to have him back, no longer as a slave but as a brother Christian. Such is the revolutionary power of the gospel, even in the most heavily structured social situations.

Paul prefaces action by prayer. Once again we have the themes of remembering and gratitude for all that the Lord has already done in building his love and faith into Philemon's character. Once again the emphasis is that real love towards Jesus must show itself by equally real love towards others. But what does Paul actually seek in his prayer for his colleague? "Partnership", *koinōnia,* is the key word in all transactions between fellow believers. We share a common Lord, faith and blessings. Here, Paul is trusting that the strength of that common faith and love which unite himself and Philemon in Christ will be powerful enough to embrace a runaway slave who has also found the same faith and love in Jesus. Paul longs for him to set the man free, but in this most subtle and delicate letter he refrains from specifically asking that. Instead he prefers to pray that their common trust in the liberating grace of the Lord Jesus, and deep insight into all the good things he wants for his followers, will be so strong in Philemon that he comes to understand that before God we are all Onesimuses.

What a way to pray for colleagues! Sometimes we have hard things to ask them, and are wondering if we should. Sometimes they are in difficult circumstances and do not know what they should do. Fellowship is the key. We need to revel in the participation we jointly have in Christ, and pray that the knowledge of this may be so strong in them that God will be able to guide them with great clarity towards what they should do. How much better than praying what *we* think is best for them to do. Paul is concerned that what *Jesus* thinks best should emerge, certain that this will further lead to Christ's blessing.

> *Dear Lord, we thank you for the forgiveness, faith and blessings*
> *we share with our fellow believers. May the love we have for you*
> *unite us, so that we may work together for your glory. Amen.*

# PART 5

# Prayer for the Growing Church

# Praying for the Ephesians

## DAY 47: LOST IN WONDER, LOVE AND PRAISE

> To the saints in Ephesus, the believers who are in Christ Jesus
> ... Praise be to the God and Father of our Lord Jesus Christ.
>
> Ephesians 1:1–3

We now find Paul praying for Christians at large. This may not be altogether obvious, because we find his prayer in the first chapter of Ephesians, which looks as if it was directed to one specific church. This is, however, probably not the case. For one thing, the words "in Ephesus" in this salutation are missing from a number of early manuscripts. Further, the letter has no reference to the work in Ephesus, where Paul spent three years, or to individuals in the church there. And it was known in some circles as the "Letter to the Laodiceans".

We can imagine that it did indeed go to Ephesus, but also to cities like Miletus, Laodicea and others in the western part of the Province of Asia. Ephesians is a companion piece to Colossians, written by Paul in prison, at the same time, dealing with the same great themes, and conveyed by the same messenger, Tychicus. It shows the origin and development of the church of Christ beginning to be established worldwide.

So how does Paul pray for Christians as they become a significant factor across the world? This extended prayer of Ephesians 1 seems to fall into three sections, the first of which is heartfelt praise (vv. 3 – 14). Three great themes are interwoven in these verses: "in Christ" comes twelve times; "according to the purpose of his will" comes three times; and "to the praise of his glory" recurs three times. They denote, respectively, the nature, the origin and the purpose of our lives. How complete and far-reaching this gospel is that they, and we, have received!

We are privileged to overhear a saint of God pouring out his heart in praise for this undreamed-of generosity of God's good news, which has made new men and women of people all over the Roman Empire – and still does throughout the world today. Until we ourselves have some experience of becoming lost in wonder, love and praise, we shall not progress very far in the school of prayer.

*Father God, I praise you for your purposes which existed before time, through the people of Israel, in the early church, and which continue today and far beyond – that we have an eternal gospel which gives us meaningful lives and hope for the future. May I always keep this sense of wonder at your great gospel plan. Amen.*

*Paul's Praise*

## Day 48: Praise for God's incalculable blessings

Praise be to [or, *blessed be*] the God and Father of our Lord Jesus Christ, who has blessed us in the heavenly realms with every spiritual blessing in Christ.

Ephesians 1:3

One of the most remarkable things in this initial part of Paul's prayer is the way in which the praise is centred upon God himself. In the New Testament, God is often addressed as "Blessed". People are blessed when they receive his blessings; God is blessed when men and women receive his generosity with love and thankfulness. Paul expands this blessing of verse 3 into a sevenfold blessing which God has poured out on all Christians the world over, for which he wants to give God the glory and praise that are his due.

First, we see in this verse that *God has blessed us* with "every spiritual blessing" which lies wrapped up "in Christ". The wealth of these blessings is incalculable. The nature of these blessings is "spiritual", as opposed to the material wealth which often marked God's goodness in Old Testament times. And the time at which these blessings became available was at our first connection with

Christ, when we "received him" or were "baptised into him". He has blessed us with them already. It is up to us to draw upon the blessings of Christ, of which we are only dimly aware.

What an astounding thought! All the blessings God intends for us are latent in the Christ with whom all Christians are already connected. There is no second (or hundredth) blessing which can be added on top of him. These blessings simply make real in our experience what God intended for us when we first became Christians. No wonder Paul is almost tongue-tied in praise. And just as he mentions "blessing" three times in this opening verse, he insists three times in the ensuing verses that we too are to live "to the praise of his glory". The reciprocity of his generosity and our responsive lifestyle could hardly be more clearly stated.

*Blessed Lord, I thank you for the wealth of spiritual blessings that you have made available to us in Christ. Show me how to draw upon them so that I may live fully to your praise and glory. Amen.*

# DAY 49: ADORATION FOR GOD'S COSTLY GENEROSITY

> For he chose us in him before the creation of the world to be holy and blameless in his sight. In love he predestined us for adoption to sonship through Jesus Christ, in accordance with his pleasure and will – to the praise of his glorious grace, which he has freely given us in the One he loves. In him we have redemption through his blood, the forgiveness of sins, in accordance with the riches of God's grace that he lavished on us.
>
> Ephesians 1:4–8

*P*aul continues to unfold the nature of the blessings we have in Christ.

The second of these is that *God has chosen us*. What an encouragement that is. To be sure, we chose him. But with the benefit of hindsight we can see that he set his love upon us and chose us long before we were ever in the position to respond. Paul goes on to reflect on the reasons why God chose us: that we should be "blameless" – with nothing held against us; that we should be "holy" – his people; and that we should be "in his sight" and "in [his] love". Then indeed we shall be to the praise of his glory. Paul exults in the vision and generosity of such a God.

Third, *God has adopted us*. It is as if we were street kids with a criminal record, and God in his love not only paid our fines and cleared our names, but adopted us into his own family alongside his one and only Son. What love that bespeaks! What confidence and freedom that gives! He has chosen us, even us, to be in his family.

Fourth, *God has rescued us* from the accusing load of our wrongdoings. "Redemption" is an evocative word. To the Hebrew it would have meant rescue from guilt and alienation from God through a blood sacrifice. To the Greek it would have brought to mind mental images of slaves being set free from bondage after they had been bought by a new master. That freeing from the guilt and slavery of evil was immensely costly. It cost our Lord no less than "the forgiveness of sins" which was achieved "through his blood" on the cross. The cross of Christ takes us to the very heart of God and causes even the angels to bow their heads in adoration.

> *My Saviour and Redeemer, I thank you that you set your love on me and my fellow Christians long ago. I praise you that your unfathomable purpose is to make us holy and blameless, set free from our countless sins by the sacrifice of your own Son on the cross. Amen.*

# DAY 50: CONFIDENCE IN GOD'S GREAT DESIGN

> With all wisdom and understanding, he made known to us
> the mystery of his will according to his good pleasure, which
> he purposed in Christ, to be put into effect when the times
> reach their fulfilment – to bring unity to all things in heaven
> and on earth under Christ. In him we were also chosen, hav-
> ing been predestined according to the plan of him who works
> out everything in conformity with the purpose of his will, in
> order that we, who were the first to put our hope in Christ,
> might be for the praise of his glory.
>
> Ephesians 1:8–12

*Y*ou might think that these four blessings were enough.
But the apostle offers two more!

Fifth, in his blessing, *God has enlightened us.* Jesus Christ, in
whom we are incorporated, is the key to life, to reality, to the
whole universe. All will, one day, find fulfilment in him, the cosmic Christ. He is "the steward of the fullness of the times" (v. 10,
Greek), and he will bring all that is in heaven and all that is on
earth into a final harmony. It is impossible for us to imagine how
this can be, or even what it could mean – but then it would have
been no less possible for us to conceive of Jew and Gentile being
united in a single "body of Christ", or graceless rebels being reconciled with a holy God. Both have come about through Christ.
That gives us great confidence that at the end of all things he will
indeed have the final reconciling word.

Sixth, *God has acquired us.* The God who works everything
out after the purpose of his own will destined us as his "inheritance" *(klēros).* The God who fashioned the universe wants only

this for his inheritance – the total loyalty and loving response of reconciled sinners like us. It would be marvellous enough to think that we have God for our inheritance, but that is not what is uppermost in the apostle's mind. He is awestruck with the thought that *we are God's inheritance!* The question for us might be: "Is he enjoying his inheritance? Or are we robbing him?"

This is our God. This is his great design. He knew what he was doing. He planned it. He has the power to bring it about. Praise God! We shall indeed, one day, "be for the praise of his glory".

> *Loving Creator God, I thank you that you revealed your reconciling will to us through Christ, that we have a future hope, and that you want nothing more than to keep us in you for the praise of your glory. Amen.*

# Day 51: Confidence in God's seal

> And you also were included in Christ when you heard the
> word of truth, the gospel of your salvation. When you
> believed, you were marked in him with a seal, the promised
> Holy Spirit, who is a deposit guaranteeing our inheritance
> until the redemption of those who are God's possession – to
> the praise of his glory.
>
> Ephesians 1:13–14

*F*inally, in Paul's sevenfold description of blessing, *God has
sealed us* with his Holy Spirit. The Holy Spirit, promised long
ago in Joel and Ezekiel, has been graciously distributed, ever since
Pentecost, to all members of the Lord's family who have heard and
believed. Paul sees the Spirit as having two special functions.

First, he is a "seal", and the seal is always, in antiquity, the
mark of ownership. You marked your letter with your personal
stamp. You sealed your sheep with a special branding iron. You
intended others to know who owned them. And it is like that
with God. He gives us his Holy Spirit so that it should be obvious to all that there is something different about us. We are his
property, his possession.

The other word the apostle uses here, "deposit", is no less significant. The Spirit is seen as a down payment, a first instalment,
of all God's future blessings for us. We do not have everything God
is planning for us yet, but we do have the pledge, the guarantee of
God's future in the Holy Spirit who lives within us. Heaven lies
beyond our vision, but a little bit of heaven is inside our
hearts – the Holy Spirit. He is the proof that the Lord will come
back one day to claim his own. It is hardly surprising that in modern Greek the word used here, *arrabōn,* means engagement ring,

the pledge of a blissful future. No wonder Paul ends once again with awestruck love: "to the praise of his glory".

This first part of Paul's amazing prayer teaches us the prime importance of praise. Let us give priority to praising God. It is one of the clearest evidences of being sealed by the Spirit of God. And it is the only proper response of creatures before their Creator, and of ransomed sinners before their Saviour. Praise the Lord!

*Holy Lord, once again I stand in awe that your Spirit – promised thousands of years ago and made manifest at Pentecost – lives in me, marking me as your own and guaranteeing heaven to me. I can only praise you, Lord! Amen.*

*Paul's Prayer*

## DAY 52: PRAYER THAT THEIR HEARTS BE ENLIGHTENED

> For this reason, ever since I heard about your faith in the Lord
> Jesus and your love for all God's people, I have not stopped
> giving thanks for you, remembering you in my prayers. I keep
> asking that the God of our Lord Jesus Christ, the glorious
> Father, may give you the Spirit of wisdom and revelation, so
> that you may know him better. I pray that the eyes of your
> heart may be enlightened in order that you may know the
> hope to which he has called you.
>
> Ephesians 1:15–18

"For this reason" – knowing we are God's heirs, knowing
we belong, knowing he set his love on us long before we
ever responded, knowing we believe, knowing we are destined for
his heavenly home – it is time to pray! "Faith in the Lord Jesus"
and "love for all God's people" is a very passable description of the
authentic Christian life. So Paul launches into petition for his
readers, that they may become what in God's purposes they
already are. Notice what he asks: not for things, but for people;
not for possessions, but for character. The cry of his heart is,
"Lord, make them understand."

Paul is afraid that they have buried treasure in their garden, barrels of the choicest food, but they do not know it, and they survive on husks. So he asks for wisdom, for perception, for deep knowledge *(epignōsis)* of Jesus, so that the eyes of their hearts may be enlightened. Notice that he does not say, "the eyes of their minds". It is all too possible to have the most immaculate theological insights and yet be blind to the realities of what the Lord offers us. It is not only our minds that need his touch, but also our blind hearts.

What, then, does Paul long to see them understand? First, *the hope of God's calling.* The call is in the past, and they have responded to it. But what they hope for lies in the future, and they have not yet attained it. The call of God brings to people without hope (Eph. 2:12) a confident assurance of a future dominated by God himself. Confidence in that future should have a profound shaping effect upon our lives. Paul would agree with John's words on the matter:

> See what great love the Father has lavished on us, that we should be called children of God. And that is what we are! . . . Dear friends, now we are children of God, and he has not yet appeared. But we know that when Christ appears, we shall be like him, for we shall see him as he is. All who have this hope in him purify themselves, just as he is pure.
>
> 1 John 3:1–3

*Glorious Father, I thank you for the new Christians that I know, whom you have made alive in your Spirit. Please give them wisdom and knowledge of yourself, so that they may be confident in the future they have in you in this life and in heaven, when we will all be made like your Son. Amen.*

# DAY 53: PRAYER THAT THEY WOULD ENTER INTO THEIR INHERITANCE

> In order that you may know ... the riches of his glorious
> inheritance in the saints, and his incomparably great power
> for us who believe. That power is like the working of his
> mighty strength, which he exerted in Christ when he raised
> him from the dead.
>
> Ephesians 1:18–20

*P*aul longs that his readers should understand *the wealth of God's inheritance.* The inheritance God gives to us as Christians is something which we only gradually understand, just as our eyes might slowly adjust to a brilliant sunlit landscape after being imprisoned in a gloomy cave for years. As we are enlightened by the Holy Spirit, the first instalment of that inheritance, we come to see more and more of the wonder of what we are invited to share: the inheritance of God himself, which we share with his Son Jesus Christ. There is nothing starry-eyed about all this. Paul knows well that suffering is an inescapable part of our lot, as it was of Christ's. But he is no less sure that glory lies at the end of the road:

> Now if we are children, then we are heirs – heirs of God and
> co-heirs with Christ, if indeed we share in his sufferings in
> order that we may also share in his glory. I consider that our
> present sufferings are not worth comparing with the glory that
> will be revealed in us.
>
> Rom. 8:17–18

How better could one pray for friends in Christ than that they may grow in appreciation of their inheritance, and come to enter more fully into all that God has in store for them?

Paul prays that they would understand *the greatness of God's power.* The power of God is the great present reality we need to engage, fulfilling the past calling and leading on to the future inheritance. Once again Paul leaves us speechless with his prayer. His heart's desire is that his readers may know nothing less than the power of the resurrection itself in their lives, a supernatural power beyond anything we human beings could attain by our unaided efforts. It is the very power of God himself, the power which raised Christ from the tomb on the first Easter Day.

What a thing to realise in our own lives. What a thing to pray for our friends. So often we trudge around with our eyes on the ground and little expectation of help from God in changing habits and attitudes, or dealing with inner hurts in our lives – when all the time the boundless power of the resurrection is waiting to be unleashed in us, if only we would make the connection of prayer!

> *Almighty God, I praise you that you have brought us, your children, out into the brilliant sunlit landscape of your inheritance. May we lift our eyes to see the future glory we will share with you and, by your grace, recognise more of your resurrection power for our lives now. Amen.*

# Paul's Contemplation

## DAY 54: TAKEN UP WITH HIS BELOVED

> In order that you may know ... the mighty strength he exerted
> when he raised Christ from the dead and seated him at his
> right hand in the heavenly realms, far above all rule and
> authority, power and dominion, and every name that can be
> invoked, not only in the present age but also in the one to
> come.
>
> Ephesians 1:18–21

As Paul lies in prison, all thoughts of those he has been praying for fade away. He is caught up with Christ in God. He has eyes only for Jesus, the one whom God raised to vindicate his claims and achievements; Jesus who is now accorded by God the Father the highest honour in the cosmos. Paul is totally taken up with his Beloved, and that is the nature of true contemplation.

He sees Jesus as *crowned King,* and bows in wonder at his feet. The exaltation of the king of Israel as God's anointed in the vision of Psalm 110:1 is fulfilled in the exaltation of Jesus after his work on earth is accomplished: "The LORD says to my Lord: 'Sit at my right hand until I make your enemies a footstool for your feet.'"

Paul also sees Jesus as the *ultimate victor,* "far above all rule ..." He is alluding here to the views of Gnostics who thought of a kind

of ladder of intermediary powers between the material world and
God. He asserts, with sublime confidence because of the cross and
resurrection, that Jesus is victor over all of them. His is the name
above every name, and at the end all will have to bow to it and
acknowledge that Jesus is Lord, to the glory of God the Father (see
Phil. 2:9–11). Paul needs no bidding to bow and confess Christ's
Lordship now!

> *Victorious Lord, may you be honoured and praised by all people*
> *everywhere for the accomplishment of your saving work. I bow*
> *before you, God's anointed King, sovereign over all the powers of*
> *this world. Amen.*

# DAY 55: BROUGHT TO CHRIST'S FEET IN AWE

> And God placed all things under his feet and appointed him
> to be head over everything for the church, which is his body,
> the fulness of him who fills everything in every way.
>
> Ephesians 1:22–23

Paul sees Jesus as the *perfect man*, and his mind goes to Psalm 8:

> When I look at thy heavens, the work of thy fingers,
>     the moon and the stars which thou hast established;
> what is man that thou art mindful of him,
>     and the son of man that thou dost care for him?
> Yet thou hast made him little less than God,
>     and dost crown him with glory and honour.
> Thou hast given him dominion over the works of thy hands;
>     thou hast put all things under his feet.
>
> Psalm 8:3–6 RSV

That is what man was intended to be, the glorious crown of
God's creation, living in total dependence on God and obedience
to him. But man has proved unequal to this high calling, and has
fallen into sinful rebellion. Not so for Jesus! He embodies both
perfect obedience to God and perfect sovereignty of the world
over which mankind was given dominion. Paul longs to be trans-
formed into the likeness of this Perfect Man.

Finally, Paul sees Jesus as the *head of the church*. The church is
"his body". Jesus is "the head", the source of life, the organ of sovereignty, the direction-giver to the whole body. The church is indis-
solubly linked with this exalted head. It is called to unconditional
obedience to his every wish. It is meant to be the expression of his
invisible presence, and the recipient of the fullness which he longs

to pour into his body's every limb. And in a final act of daring, Paul sees the church as something which brings fullness to Christ himself – this is how the Greek is best construed. The head has determined to be incomplete without the body. There is a profound interdependence between the church and its Lord.

This is the Jesus who fills Paul's gaze as he prays for the worldwide church of God. He is the Alpha and the Omega of all existence, and prayer properly brings us to his feet in utter awe and wonder as we contemplate his glory.

> *Sovereign Lord, I thank you for sending Jesus as the perfect man, whom one day we will model as all you intended us to be in the stewardship of the new heavens and new earth. I pray that we as your church, Christ's body, may daily depend on him and bring him honour, for the sake of your glory. Amen.*

# PART 6

# Meditation and Adoration

*Paul's Meditation*

## DAY 56: MARVELLING AT THE MYSTERY OF THE GOSPEL

> This mystery is that through the gospel the Gentiles are heirs
> together with Israel, members together of one body, and shar-
> ers together in the promise in Christ Jesus. I became a servant
> of this gospel by the gift of God's grace.
>
> Ephesians 3:6–7

The prayer in Ephesians 1 sprang from praise. The prayer
in Ephesians 3 emerges from meditation. Paul begins in
verse 1 of the chapter, "For this reason I, Paul, the prisoner of
Christ Jesus for the sake of you Gentiles – ", and then he gets dis-
tracted by the wonder of the gospel. The next twelve verses are a
meditation on this theme, and then he returns to where he left
off: "For this reason I kneel before the Father . . ."

There is nothing wrong with having distractions in our
prayers. We must not court them: that is why Jesus told us to go
into our room and shut the door when we pray. But distractions
will come whether the door is closed or not! The best way to han-
dle them is often not to fight them but to follow them, turning
them into meditation before God, or possibly intercession. That is
what Paul does here. His digression about the Gentiles is extremely

fruitful; the same can (sometimes) be said of our wandering thoughts in prayer. After all, the Lord may want us to go down that particular side alley.

As Paul mentions the word "Gentiles", he stops in his tracks and begins to marvel at the way his life has turned out. He had been the strictest type of Jew, unwilling even to spit at "Gentile dogs", lest his spit be defiled. Yet God had reached him, "less than the least of all people", with the gospel which he strove so hard to suppress. The shame of the situation bites deep into his soul – the years of hatred in his heart for Jesus and his violent excursions to kill new Christians. In the succeeding years he, Paul, was to be a prime instrument of God to reach those very same Gentiles whom he had once despised, with the gospel which he had once tried to destroy.

So he marvels at the gospel itself, the very mystery of Christ. In previous generations this mystery had lain unknown, although prophets had hinted at it. Now what was once hidden is bathed in glorious light: the Gentiles, the outsiders, are to be fellow heirs with God's chosen people, the Jews, and partners in the same promises that were made centuries earlier to Abraham and his descendants. Paul marvels at the birth of a new race, where words like "Jew" and "Gentile", so terribly divisive, cease to have meaning. The new day has come. The church has been born!

> *Christ Jesus, guide my thoughts as I meditate on you in the stillness of prayer. You are the same mighty Lord who turned around the life of Paul, and who extended to the nations your promises to Israel. I praise you that all who believe in you can inherit these eternal promises by your grace. Amen.*

# DAY 57: WONDERING AT GOD'S PERFECT PARENTHOOD

> For this reason I kneel before the Father, from whom every
> family in heaven and on earth derives its name.
>
> Ephesians 3:14

*T*his prayer is permeated by a sense of wonder at being in God's family. God had reached out to estranged Gentiles like the Ephesians and proud Jews like Paul, and had brought them both into the same divine family. Now he prays to "the Father". In his pre-Christian days he could never have addressed the High and Holy One who inhabits eternity in such a fashion. But Jesus had given to his followers the incredible privilege of addressing God in the same way as he himself did, calling him "*Abba,* dear Daddy". That word takes us to the very heart of God, our loving Father.

Paul reflects further on the Father to whom he is about to pray, from whom "any father-headed group" is derived. One commentator put it beautifully: "The name of Father did not go up from us, but from above it came to us." This is such a contrast to the ideas of Freud, whose work persuaded him that God was a projection into the untenanted heavens of our own father-image. Not many people would want their "old man" as God! There is something very different about God our Father. Our human family relations, spoiled and marred by sin and discord, are pale reflections of that perfect Parent in heaven who is the ultimate source of all love and all families.

We can pray with confidence to such a God. So could the scattered groups of Christians throughout Asia Minor, often weak, sometimes persecuted, frequently discouraged, whom Paul exhorts not to lose heart but to make use of their right of access to the Father.

> *Loving Father God, I thank you for the privilege of being a child in your divine family, born out of your loving sacrifice and free to come and talk to you in prayer. May I always rest in the assurance of your perfect parenthood. Amen.*

*Paul's Petition*

## DAY 58: RECEIVING GOD'S OVERWHELMING GIFTS

> I pray that out of his glorious riches he may strengthen you
> with power through his Spirit in your inner being, so that
> Christ may dwell in your hearts through faith.
>
> Ephesians 3:16–17

Paul now prays with a deep concern for these Gentiles over whom he has been brooding. Urgency in prayer comes from his time of meditation. As he sees the wonder of what God has delighted to do in them, he is deeply concerned that they should not fail to be the salt and the light in the world that God intended.

So he prays for strength through the Spirit. He wants them to be mightily strengthened, according to God's glorious riches. The gift is overwhelming, like the love and riches of the Giver.

He also prays that Christ may dwell in their hearts through faith. Far too many church people think Christianity is something we do for God, rather than allowing him to come and minister to us. But rather than doing good and religious things, it begins with receiving a gracious, indwelling Saviour, making room for our Lord and Master in our hearts.

Paul knew that well and prayed that his readers would genuinely put their trust in Jesus, asking him to come and make his home in their lives. That is precisely what the Greek word translated "dwell" means. It means Christ will "be at home", not as a temporary resident, but in a way that means there is no place in their hearts and lives he may not go. Christians like that are going to be of some use in the world!

*Dear Lord and Master, please dwell in my heart and in the hearts of Christians everywhere. Come and minister to us. Give us overwhelming strength, according to your glorious riches, so that we may live to your praise and glory. Amen.*

# DAY 59: FILLED WITH THE LIMITLESS LOVE OF CHRIST

> And I pray that you, being rooted and established in love, may
> have power, together with all God's people, to grasp how wide
> and long and high and deep is the love of Christ, and to know
> this love that surpasses knowledge – that you may be filled to
> the measure of all the fulness of God.
>
> Ephesians 3:17–19

*Y*ou cannot have Christ in your heart without having love
on board. Just as Paul wants Jesus to be at home in the
Ephesians' lives, so he wants Jesus' love to flow over and through
them. From love to love: that is the progression of the Christian
life. We are meant to be grounded in it and growing in it. There
is no higher thing to pray for anyone, than that they may grow
in the love of God. Love is the language of heaven; it is the very
nature of the Trinity.

Because the God we worship is unity in plurality, the experience of Christian love is of the same kind. It is not in lonely culti-
vation of our souls, but "with all God's people" that we begin to
grasp the love of God which defies language. We see this love in
some people; we feel it when we are in their presence – and God
wants his children to emanate that warmth and light of love. But we
cannot give it out until we take it in, and the apostle prays that his
readers may have the strength to do just that, and comprehend the
sheer dimensions of the love of Jesus which has loved them into life.

The *length* to which the love of God is willing to go is limitless: "he is able to save completely those who come to God
through him, because he always lives to intercede for them" (Heb.
7:25). The *breadth* of God's love is shown by Christ being "the

atoning sacrifice for our sins, and not only for ours but also for the sins of the whole world" (1 John 2:2). And what of the *depth* of Christ's love? "For you know the grace of our Lord Jesus Christ, that though he was rich, yet for your sakes he became poor, so that you through his poverty might become rich" (2 Cor. 8:9). And the *height* of it? Well, "because of his great love for us, God, who is rich in mercy, made us alive with Christ even when we were dead in transgressions . . . And God raised us up with Christ and seated us with him in the heavenly realms" (Eph. 2:4 – 6).

Such is the generosity of our Lord Jesus Christ. May we make the indweller so much at home in our lives that his love will overflow into every corner, so that we are "filled to the measure of all the fulness of God" (v. 19) – and what is that, but love?

> *Heavenly Lord, I am overwhelmed by your infinite, saving love which has raised us up with Christ. I pray that those I know and love may also be grounded in your love, that we may together emanate your warmth and light, being filled to the measure of your fullness. Amen.*

# Paul's Adoration

## DAY 60: PRAISE THAT ECHOES THROUGHOUT TIME AND ETERNITY

> Now to him who is able to do immeasurably more than all we ask or imagine, according to his power that is at work within us, to him be glory in the church and in Christ Jesus throughout all generations, for ever and ever! Amen.
>
> Ephesians 3:20–21

Paul ends this marvellous prayer with adoring commitment to the Lord to whom he prays. Nobody has ever framed a bolder prayer than the one Paul has just prayed: that his readers be filled with all the fullness of God. And yet this apostle, who has the abiding power to surprise us, does it yet again. He triumphantly invokes a power which is able to do a great deal more than he asks.

Look at the *promise he claims:* God is able to do abundantly more than all we can ask or think. There is no limit to his power. It soars above all we can ask or even imagine. And here is this prayer warrior in his filthy cell, utterly convinced that nothing – *nothing* – is too hard for his God. That is the sort of faith that the living God delights to answer. It does not only request, but exhibits "his power at work within us".

Now look at the *sequel he envisages.* The culmination of his prayer and meditation is simple: glory should be ascribed to the God and Father of our Lord Jesus Christ for ever. Glory to him in the church. Glory to him in the Saviour. This is the goal of Paul's vision. God is all in all, and his praise echoes throughout time and eternity. At the furthest horizon of our imagination we see Jesus and his people rendering to the Father in heaven that unceasing glory and praise which is his due.

What a man of prayer we find in Saul of Tarsus! But he would not be interested in our admiration. He would say to us tersely, as he did to the Thessalonians: "Pray without ceasing!"

*Almighty and Eternal Lord, I follow Paul's example in praising you for your limitless power at work in the lives of your people. I pray that I may continue to walk closely with you, and that your church may give you unceasing glory through Christ Jesus. Amen.*